ALL-AMERICAN® WONDER

ALL-AMERICAN® WONDER

VOLUME II

INFORMATION REGARDING THE HISTORY, PRODUCTION, FEATURES AND THE RESTORATION OF MILITARY JEEPS 1941 - 1945

by

Ray Cowdery

with

Merrill Madsen

Illustrated by Ray Cowdery

Library of Congress Cataloging in Publication Data
USM, Inc.
International Standard Book Number (ISBN) 0-910667-20-9

Cowdery, Ray R. 1941 -

Title: **All-American Wonder, Volume II**
              Third (1999) American Edition

1. AUTOMOBILES, Military Vehicles, History, Repairing, Restoring
2. HISTORY, Automobiles, Military Vehicles, World War II

Printed in Hong Kong.

DISTRIBUTED EXCLUSIVELY WORLDWIDE BY:

USM Incorporated, PO Box 2600, Rapid City, SD 57709-2600 USA
Fax: (605) 341-5488

*Notice that our address and fax number were changed in November 1997.
Please correct your records.*

MILITARY VEHICLE / AUTO INTEREST BOOKS PUBLISHED BY USM, INC. INCLUDE:

All-American Wonder, volume I (1993 revision)	ISBN 0-910667-10-1
All-American Wonder, volume II (1999 edition)	ISBN 0-910667-20-9
Selling the All-American Wonder	ISBN 0-910667-25-X
Willys MB Master Parts List TM 10-1186	ISBN 0-910667-11-X
Willys MB Maintenance Manual TM 10-1513	ISBN 0-910667-16-0
Ford Master Parts List SNL G-658	ISBN 0-910667-18-7
Willys-Overland MB Chassis Print Set (3 quarter-scale drawings)	A-2981
James Sessions Jeep Prints (8 full color prints)	A-2908-X
Major Items and Combinations, Automotive ORD 3 SNL G-1	ISBN 0-910667-15-2
Ford GP Master Parts List TM 1100	ISBN 0-910667-17-9
Modern Ordnance Materiel (Raritan Manual 1943)	ISBN 0-910667-30-6
Dein KdF Wagen (Your Volkswagen) 1939	ISBN 0-910667-39-X
1929 Auto Owners Supply Book (Western Auto)	ISBN 0-910667-03-9

Order from your favorite bookstore or internet bookseller. If not available, write or fax USM at the address in the box above.

This book is Volume II of a two volume set of books on the subject of standard production MBs and GPWs of the World War II era. Volume I is entirely different book than Volume II, and together the two volumes are the most comprehensive study of the subject available in the American language. Volume I was translated into Japanese by Yasuo Ohtsuka in 1986. Volume II was translated into the Czech language in 1993 by Peter Vodenka.

1941 - 1945

ALL - AMERICAN ● WONDER

© COPYRIGHT 1986
RRC

The name "Jeep" with a capital J is a trademark of Jeep-Eagle Corporation, a part of Chrysler Corporation. The word "jeep" with a lower case j as used in this book is the generic form as found in many dictionaries. Our authority for use is *Webster's Seventh New Collegiate Dictionary*, G. & C. Merriam Company, Springfield, MA, USA, various editions. We quote:

jeep/'jēp/*n*: a small general purpose motor vehicle with 80 inch wheelbase, ¼ ton capacity, and four-wheel drive used by the US Army in WWII.

Jeep *trademark* - used for small vehicle similar to an army jeep . . . .

"Peeps" of the First Armored Division, U. S. A., in action at Fort Knox, K;

FOREWORD

To a very large number of uninformed people any jeep is simply "a jeep". A lot of them erroneously call any open, 4 wheel drive vehicle a jeep. Those same people probably can't distinguish between an Arabian and an Appaloosa, or tell a Volkswagen from a V-2 either. The purpose of *All-American Wonder, Volume II* is to bring additional definition to the various models of jeeps produced between 1941 and 1945 and to broaden the field of knowledge about them.

The jeep was first designed and produced in response to the US Army request for bids (dated 27 June 1940) for command/reconnaissance cars with an 80 inch wheelbase, and weighing 1300 pounds. Those who delivered prototypes for testing at Camp Holabird, Maryland were Bantam (23 September 1940), Willys-Overland (11 November 1940) and Ford (23 November 1940). The prototypes, the Bantam Reconnaissance Car, Ford "Pygmy" and the Willys "Quad" proved that the concept was correct and the government asked that all three manufacturers make production runs of 1500 improved vehicles for further testing.

The vehicles delivered on these orders were the Bantam BRC-40, the Ford GP and the Willys MA. The 2,675 produced by Bantam were to be the last jeeps they would ever make. Ford made 5,756 GPs and Willys built 1,555 MAs and 25,808 MB "Slat Grills" before the government standardized on the Willys MB and the Ford version of the same vehicle, the GPW. Some 612,145 of these standardized jeeps were built before WWII ended.

Prior to the end of WWII, Willys-Overland had already modified 26 MBs into what was to become the CJ-2A, the first civilian version of the famous jeep. Together with the CJ-3A and CJ-3B these were the last "Jeep" vehicles based on the original classic version.

The response to *All-American Wonder, Volume I* clearly indicated that students, collectors and restorers of military jeeps simply cannot get enough information. Knowing that some jeeps used 6.00 x 16 inch tires is not enough--jeep enthusiasts want virtually every last detail about those tires, the tubes that went in them, the pumps that put air in them and even the

gauges that monitored their inflation pressure.

I always thought I was peculiar when I sought this sort of detailed information. I've learned I'm not alone. I may indeed be peculiar but if I am, thousands of others are as well. During the years that I was involved with Willys MPLS, a jeep parts supplier, I spent a part of everyday disassembling jeeps or parts, reading manuals and sales literature or comparing piles of seemingly similar parts. This was a real luxury that few hobbiests have access to. I was able to observe a quantity of material that few people would ever see, and the quality and originality of that material was excellent. Many of the jeeps we dragged in came out of the northwoods and had never been cannibalized for parts.

The situation at Willys MPLS was made even more valuable because of the daily conversations I was able to have with Tom and Louis Larson and Merrill Madsen. All three are "peculiar" in the jeep sense. Then there were the customers who came for replacement parts. People like Joe

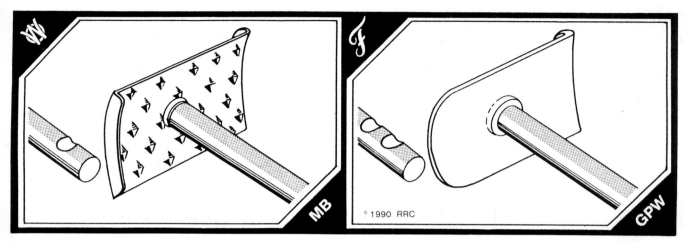

Typical Willys clutch and brake pedals are stamped steel while Ford used a cast iron pedal pinned to the shaft. The Ford version also came with two grooves in the shaft so the pitch could be adjusted.

Houdak, Bob Dahl, Pat Stene, Gary Nelson, Larry Smith and Rick Anderson always pointed out the latest jeep oddity they had uncovered.

I don't want to suggest that this circumstance led to one human "knowing it all" about jeeps. Quite the contrary; I've heard *each* of the people mentioned above state that *the more they learned about jeeps, the more obvious their limited knowledge became.* I feel the same way. Almost every question answered spawns a couple more questions. The result of my situation was that I was able to accumulate and record detail information that nobody could be expected to remember.

A great deal of material has been acquired that could not be used in this book. I have decided that the subject of military jeeps is worth persuing farther and I am currently working on separate monographs covering:

Prototype jeeps	The MB
The MA	The GPW
The GP	The CJs
The BRC-40	The M-38

These monographs *will not* be published in sequence. Each will provide a lot of information and photos of one specific model and each will contain 8 pages of color photos. If you have information you think would be of value in one or more of these monographs, please write me at the Lakeville, MN USA address on the back of the title page of this book. All contributions used will be acknowledged in the books.

THANKS TO MANY . . . . . .

It was a great deal easier to write volume II of this book than it was to write volume I. I had a lot more help. People from all over the world sent me data, information, photos and opinions that have been used to make this book a better, more accurate and more useful product.

I am proud of my work but am more proud of those who unselfishly lent what they had with no objective other than to make it available to jeep freaks everywhere. I hope that all that helped will find their name on the list that follows. I apologize to any who I may have overlooked. My special thanks to Yasuo Ohtsuka who translated Volume I into Japanese and nursed the manuscript through production.

I have done what I can do for MB and GPW owners around the world. It is my sincere hope that others will continue to solve the many puzzles that remain about these wonderful little trucks, and publish their works so that I may buy them.

Thanks to:

MERRILL MADSEN
DARCY MILLER
TONY SUDDS
YASUO OHTSUKA

AND....

J ARNOLD	JOE HUDAK	SANDY STANTON
KAREN BEACH	ROBERT S JOHNSON	MIKE STOPFORTH
JEAN-LUC BEGHIN	B JONES	BRYCE SUNDERLIN
JAN BREKELMANS	BILL JUNKER	BOB THELANDER
GERARD BUNGE	DOMINIC KAUKAS	JIRI TRNKA
FRED COLDWELL	VAL KOLISEK	FRANZ UCKO
JIM COOLBAUGH	GERO KOLLER	BART VANDERVEEN
DAVID R CORE	HUBERT MEPLAIN	JOSEPHINE VAN NIEROP
BRIAN COWDERY	L MEYER	ROY VAN WICKLIN
TIM COWDERY	LAWRENCE NABHOLTZ	C TH VERSCHURE
PIETRO CRISPO	JOSEF NEMETH	JOHN VETTER
A W DU BOIS	BRIAN NERI	J J WILSON
TOM EVANS	ROBERT V NOTMAN	MILAN ZIMEL
JOHN FLAKE	C J ORCHARD	
LOUIS J FLECKENSTEIN	W STERLING PARKERSON	and TUSTIN ELLISON who ordered the very first copy.
BRIAN FRENCH	JOHAN PRIEM	
GUS GOWERS	GEORGE RABUS	
RICHARD L GRACE	HAROLD RATZBURG	
JIM GRAHAM	JAAP RIETVELD	
HARTMUT HAGNER	GLENN E SMITH	
ROY HARRIS	LARRY SMITH	
CARROLL HIGDEM	IVAN SCHATZKA	
REG HODGSON	DENNIS SPENCE	

These people contributed new information to volume II and corrected many inaccuracies, errors and errors of omission in volume I. I am very grateful. As one writer, Bryce Sunderlin, pointed out, "...once an error is committed to print, it becomes Holy Writ". Unfortunately, that is all too true. I call your attention to the corrections to volume I on the last page of this book. If you have a copy of volume I, please photocopy the last page and *glue* it in your volume I. That should go a long way to preventing the errors from becoming "Holy Writ".

Author's apology: I'm sorry I couldn't figure out a way to make this a pretty book - the kind that win awards and look nice when people open them. I decided early-on to abandon art for the sake of content. I couldn't even find a reasonable way to index this book.

Because of the wide variety of subject matter I found no way to go from chassis information in one section to electrical information in a subsequent section, etc. as is usual in this sort of book. To get it all in and to keep the price as low as possible, all kinds of information is dispersed throughout the book.

As a result, it will be necessary for the reader to read the whole book to get the most from it. That is probably not all bad. After Volume I of *All-American Wonder* was published it became obvious that many people did not read page 10 very thoroughly. I still get lots of questions about American Central composite bodies that were used on the final series of both Ford and Willys jeep production. The composite body information is essential to a reasonable understanding of the differences in jeep bodies, especially those made in the last half of WWII production.

Ray Cowdery
Lakeville, MN
55044-0810 USA

A LITTLE MORE ON THE NAME JEEP...

Although the volume of literature regarding the jeep continues to grow there is no more certainty today where the name jeep came from than there was 45 years ago.

Several things are certain:

- The comic strip character JEEP made his first appearance in papers all over America on 1 April 1936. The strip was "Popeye" by Elzie Crisler Segar.

- Haliburton Oil Well Company of Duncan, Oklahoma built a truck called Jeep in 1938.

- Minneapolis-Moline Power Implement Company called their Artillery Prime Mover a Jeep in 1940.

- Both Ford and Bantam sources take credit for the name jeep.

- Willys ended up with the trade name "Jeep" after WWII.

- The name jeep may have come from an attempt to pronounce the letters GP, but GP *never* stood for "General Purpose" as so many sources state. In the Ford Parts Numbering System, G always referred *only* to a unit built for the Government and P referred *only* to an 80 inch wheel-base reconnaissance car. The "General Purpose" idea refuses to die in spite of proof positive to the contrary.

- The most recent in a long line of owners of the "Jeep" trade name is Jeep Eagle Corporation, a part of Chrysler Motors. Amazingly, they are now trying to get the word jeep removed from dictionaries in an effort to shore-up their rights to the use of the word.

Where will it all end? It is doubtful that lexacographers will let Chrysler remove the word jeep from any dictionary and it is certain they will never remove it from popular speech anywhere. I doubt that any etymologist will ever establish a more likely origin for the word than those already put forward. Like the little WWII ¼ tons themselves, the name will always be shrouded in at least a little bit of mystery.

The original JEEP on maneuvers at Camp Ripley in 1940. The driver is James T. O'Brien who named it—he is now a Sergeant in the U. S. Army.

A CONVERTED MM FARM TRACTOR WAS THE FIRST MILITARY VEHICLE TO BE CALLED THE JEEP

The name JEEP was first given to an Army tractor by a Minnesota National Guardsman in the summer of 1940, and is not a contraction of the two words "General Purpose" (GP) but was taken from the Popeye cartoons. The author of the cartoon created a character called the Jeep which knew all the answers and could do many unusual things.

As far back as 1938, Minneapolis-Moline began working on the conversion of a farm tractor into a military vehicle for pulling big guns and other heavy equipment. After undergoing numerous field tests beginning in the spring of 1939, four experimental models of this tractor were assigned to units of the Minnesota National Guard taking part in Army Maneuvers at Camp Ripley, Minnesota, in August, 1940.

The credit for naming the new tractors goes to James T. O'Brien of the 109th Ordnance Company of the National Guard. He decided that it should be called a "Jeep," after the comic strip character, because it couldn't be definitely classified as either a truck, or a tractor, or a tank, or a caterpillar, but rather was a combination of all of these, and it could do many unusual things and literally knew all the answers. When the MM military tractors went to the Army Proving Grounds at Aberdeen, Md., in the fall of 1940, the name Jeep went with them.

The original Jeep was a 4 wheel drive machine, which is referred to in the Army as a 4 by 4. It had a 7500 pound pull on the drawbar, and was capable of travelling up to 40 miles per hour on the highway. It had a roller bumper in front, by which it could pass over solid obstructions, and a hydraulic lifting device in the rear by which the drawbar of a heavy gun, etc., could be lifted to tractor drawbar level for hitching.

Since the original MM Jeep, Minneapolis-Moline has designed several additional models of Military tractors in cooperation with Army and Navy officials. Several models of MM Jeeps are now being produced in quantity for the Armed Forces of the United Nations.

One of the models of the JEEP produced by MM for the Armed Forces.

Below: MM 6 wheel JEEP pulling an Anti-Aircraft gun.

A page from the 1944 Minneapolis-Moline calendar (printed in 1943) makes a case for their claim to the name JEEP. On the facing page is one of their full page magazine ads having the same purpose. When the lawyers got done Willys-Overland had the rights to the trademark.

But our light won't stay UNDER the Bushel...

Personal credit for naming the Jeep goes to James T. O'Brien of the 109th Ordnance Co., Minnesota National Guards, shown here driving the Jeep at Camp Ripley, Minnesota, during the 1940 maneuvers.

THE *Original* "JEEP" a child of Minneapolis Moline

True, the penalty of being imitated attaches to all leadership; but giving credit where credit is due remains a sterling principle even in wartime. Current national publicity has obscured the fact that the first war machine named "JEEP" was born at Minneapolis-Moline and christened at Camp Ripley, Minnesota (with apologies to Ripley—"Believe it or not").

Back in 1938 Minneapolis-Moline engineers were already experimenting with the conversion of a farm tractor to an artillery prime mover; and in 1940, collaborating with Adjutant General E. A. Walsh, Commander of Minn. National Guard, models were tested in maneuvers at Camp Ripley.

This new MM army vehicle was not a crawler tractor, truck nor tank, and yet it could do almost anything and it knew all the answers. Because of this, it brought to mind the Popeye cartoon figure called "JEEP" which was neither fowl nor beast, but knew all the answers and could do most anything. The National Guardsmen therefore named the MM vehicle the "JEEP". "The Jeep" name therefore is not a contraction of the term General Purpose (GP), and if it really had been, no doubt "Jeep" would have been spelled "Geep".

Since the original MM Jeep, Minneapolis-Moline has designed several additional models of Military tractors in cooperation with Army and Navy officials. Several models of MM Jeeps are now being produced in quantity for the Armed Forces of the United Nations, and in use throughout the world.

In addition, Minneapolis-Moline builds many other products for the armed forces and all the farm machinery and tractors allowed under Government limitation orders for which materials can be obtained. Minneapolis-Moline is one of very few in the United States, and the first farm machinery company, to be awarded both the Maritime "M" and the Army-Navy "E" for high quality and high production achievement.

MINNEAPOLIS-MOLINE POWER IMPLEMENT COMPANY
MINNEAPOLIS 1, MINNESOTA, U.S.A.

MM
MINNEAPOLIS-MOLINE
TRACTORS & FARM MACHINERY
MODERN FARM MACHINERY

Bantam Cars, U. S. Armored Division

...and *Peeps!*

A reproduction of a postcard purchased at the Desert Training Center, Mojave, California in July 1943 by a soldier of the 706th Tank Battalion, 37th Armored Regiment of the 4th Armored Division. Other than the jeeps shown the most interesting aspect of the card is the soldier's handwritten comment on the back that these are *"Peeps"*.

It seems that the name *Peep* was common in U S Armored units through the war. The following excerpt is from a letter dated 23 November 1944 from Colonel Charles R Codman (aide-de-camp to General George S Patton, Jr) to his wife.

"Why do I say 'peep'? I have put the question to Al who knows more about vehicles than the Chief of Ordnance."

ME: *"Al, what is the correct name for the vehicle we have been riding in all over North Africa, Sicily, England and France?"*

AL: *"The quarter-ton."*

ME: *"I see. What is a jeep?"*

AL: *"No such thing as a jeep. That's civilian talk for* any *Army vehicle. Means nothing."*

ME: *"I see. What is a peep?"*

AL: *(reluctantly) "Well, you might say it's permissable to refer to the quarter-ton as a peep -- the General (Patton) does -- but I prefer to call it by it's right name, which is the quarter-ton."*

"So, there you are, right from the horse's mouth."

I'm sure that if I had served in Patton's Third Army and *he* called them "peeps", I would too.

Here's Popeye interrogating JEEP in the comic strip of the late 1930s. JEEP was capable of unbelievable things.

SPARE WHEEL LOCK ASSEMBLY

A-1318 SPARE WHEEL LOCK NUT

A-1319

INTRODUCTION

Czechoslovakia is an unusual country. As the name implies some of the people who live there are Czechs and some are Slovaks. It is a lovely land-locked country of Hapsburgian cities with ancient centers that has produced countless world-class scientists, composers and athletes. By a curious series of events, Czechoslovakia also has more Willys MAs than any other place on earth.

For a very long time Czechoslovakians have had little to do with their own destiny. Austria ruled these people for many years; in 1938 Britain, France and Italy donated part of the country to Germany, and the Soviets kept it as a satellite for nearly half a century. In spite of the country's location among larger, stronger and more domineering neighbors, the Czechoslovak people have remained fiercely independent, patriotic and ambitious.

They struggled through 6 years of Nazi humiliation, occupation and destruction. The communist government that emerged after WWII instituted many agricultural and economic reforms that radically changed the manner in which Czechoslovakians lived. One of those affected by this turbulent history was young Jiri (Jir-zhee) Trnka, the son of a well known weapons factory owner. In May of 1945 his family got their factory back from the Nazis and laid plans to continue production of fine quality hunting guns and ammunition.

Almost immediately, Jiri took an interest in the Allied military vehicles he saw on the streets of Brno and he fell in love with jeeps. Among his long-time family friends were several Czechoslovakian foresters who were pressed into service in mid-1945 conducting an agricultural damage survey for the government. In September of 1945 the damage survey crew was the recipient of 10 jeeps provided through the United Nations Relief and Rehabilitation Administration (UNRRA) in Washington, DC, so Jiri immediately asked to drive one.

Of the 10 jeeps received by the foresters, 9 worked well and one took a liter of oil every time it went around the block. They simply parked it, and Jiri came up with an idea of his own. He mentioned to the Chief forester that his family badly needed a motor vehicle in their business and he said he'd be happy to make the oil-burning vehicle work if he could borrow it. The damage survey crew had plenty of running jeeps so they told Jiri to take the junker home.

He poured oil through the old Willys for a few months and when parts became available he fixed it. He picked up ammunition with it, he delivered weapons and he took his wife and friends for Sunday rides in it. When the damage survey was finished in

ISSUE and RECEIPT VOUCHER

NOTE—Voucher must accompany the Stores when practicable

Issue Voucher No. and Date: 879 22-10-45

Receipt Voucher No. and Date: 879 22-10-45

*For Office Stamp

Account:—

No. of Sheets .... Sheet No. ....

Issued by:—

Issued to:— CHIEF OF UNRRA MISSION PRAGUE CZECHOSLOVAKIA

Date and Mode of Conveyance: TRUCK

Carriers or Convoy Note No. and Date:

Authority for Issue			DESIGNATION (3)	Quantity (4)	Description and marks on packages (5)	For Store Depot use only.						
Ledger Folio (1)	Cat. or Part No. (2)	Section or Sub-Section				S. (6)	R. (7)	D. (8)	U. (9)	Rate (10)	Value (11) £ s. d.	
		60 TRUCKS			PARTS							
	78486-	WILLYS MODEL MA		1	SPARE PART LIST							
	98696	JEEP 1/4 TON 4X4										
		(GOVT VEHICLES)										

*Of consignor on original and triplicate, and of consignee on duplicate.

*(Signature of consignor or consignee)

Army Form G 1033 (in books of 100)

UNRRA SHIPPING RECEIPT

the summer of 1946 Jiri applied to the UNRRA to buy his jeep. The UNRRA agreed and sold it to him for 37,750 Czechoslovak Crowns, (about $755.00).

With the change of government in Czechoslovakia in 1947 the state acquired the Jan Trnka weapons factory and Jiri became a tool maker for the state tractor factory. His young daughter received her first automobile ride in the jeep and the family toured the country in it many times. In the 1950s Jiri was able to acquire the front clip from a more modern Willys and replace the square-front hood, odd fenders and the wrought iron grill on his jeep. It was not until 10 years later that Jiri Trnka realized he had converted a Willys MA into an MB.

When he realized what he had done Jiri undertook a real study of the MA. He acquired a used front clip from another MA and reinstalled it on his old "Dedek" (grandpa). He began to write to, or talk to every other MA owner on earth. He took photos, made measurements and began collecting frame plates and data plates from MAs. His son-in-law, Pavel, began to collect and restore MA instruments. The tiny jeep models Jiri makes are internationally known for their incredible detail.

When I met the Trnka family in the mid-1980s it was in their living room in central Brno. With traditional Czechoslovakian

hospitality I was treated to a big meal followed by Pilsner beer and kolackys while I went over an extremely complete collection of MA parts and information. Jiri Trnka showed me his jeep's original UNRRA manual and every receipt for every part he ever bought for it. I quickly came to doubt that anyone had owned a MA longer or loved them more than Jiri did.

The more I heard the more I realized that there were many MA mysteries that no one seemed to be able to explain. Just about everyone knows that the MA was the Willys production jeep that preceeded Willys/Ford standardization on the MB/GPW. Of the 1555 made in 1941, perhaps 35 remain (1990) and of that number 24 are in Czechoslovakia. The question is; *Why are there so many MAs in this small East-European country?*

THE CZECHOSLOVAKIAN CONNECTION

The first part of the two-part answer to the question above is easy--one could not easily export military equipment (or vehicles regarded as "cultural property") from Czechoslovakia so the old jeeps that are there tend to stay there. The second part was much more difficult--*how the MAs got to Czechoslovakia in the first place.*

At least I had some hints. The paperwork with Jiri Trnka's *"Dedek"* said the vehicle came to Czechoslovakia via the UNRRA. Jiri himself "knew" that the jeeps that came to Czechoslovakia after the war came from the West--not the East (via the Soviet Union).

During WWII the nations that formed the UN agreed to set up a relief and rehabilitation organization to feed and repatriate anticipated displaced persons and to rebuild damaged industries when the war eventually ended. Roy F Hendrickson, Administrator of the Food Distribution Administration of the US Department of Agriculture was appointed Deputy Director General for Supply at the UNRRA in Washington, DC on 16 January 1944.

The Czechoslovak civil authorities had come to agreement with the USSR in May of 1944, that upon liberation civilians would take over the administration of the country. Therefore, when the war ended there was no intervening period of military rule, but a normal transition to civil administration. The Czechoslovak government-in-exile had in the meantime (in February 1945) become one of the first Axis-occupied countries to agree to accept UNRRA aid at the conclusion of the war. The UNRRA Mission to Czechoslovakia was established in June 1945 at Kralovska 1, Praha X, with Peter I Alexejev

Jiri Trnka's MA with his dog at the wheel. The same MA at the left below in another early photograph. The MA at the right is another in the standard post-war Czechoslovakian camping configuration.

(also spelled Alekseev) as Mission Chief. It advised and disbursed supplies to the Czechoslovak office for Relief and Rehabilitation (CRR) at Petrske Nam. 1, Praha II, an office run by Dr V Schlesinger.

The UNRRA office in Washington divided their supply function into several parts: Industrial, Agricultural, Food and Medical supply divisions. On the basis of need they established budgets for recipient countries and left it to the various country Missions to help local Relief and Rehabilitation groups to decide on spending priorities. At nearly the same time the United States was trying to wind-down the greatest military over-supply situation in the history of the world. At the end of the European war the US had many divisions in Europe and enough supplies to keep them equipped for years. Millions of tons of supplies and countless vehicles littered the landscape from Africa to Norway. The Americans just wanted to go home, and they were happy to turn over their supplies to anyone that could use them. The war-torn countries of Europe and the Middle-East seemed to be likely prospects.

But history's greatest give away sounds much easier than it was in reality. On a priority basis, people wanted food, medical supplies and clothing--without fuel and drivers what would they do with trucks? Hundreds of thousands of head of livestock and poultry went to Czechoslovakia before anyone discussed trucks. Seeds for replanting, medicines, chemicals and coal were all more important than jeeps. Thousands of unguarded vehicles began to fall into disrepair in motor parks in England, France and Italy.

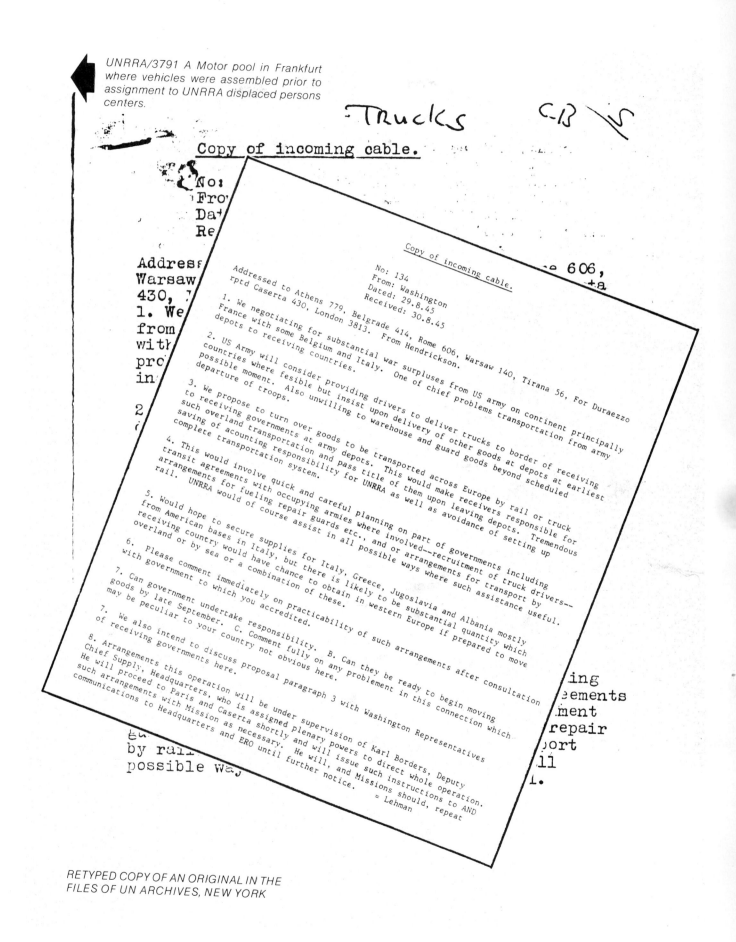

UNRRA/3791 A Motor pool in Frankfurt where vehicles were assembled prior to assignment to UNRRA displaced persons centers.

TRUCKS   C-B

Copy of incoming cable.

No:
Fro
Da
Re

Address
Warsaw
430,
1. We
from
with
pro
in

2.

Copy of incoming cable.

No: 134
From: Washington
Dated: 29.8.45
Received: 30.8.45

Addressed to Athens 779, Belgrade 414, Rome 606, Warsaw 140, Tirana 56, For Duraezzo rptd Caserta 430, London 3813. From Hendrickson.

1. We negotiating for substantial war surpluses from US army on continent principally France with some Belgium and Italy. One of chief problems transportation from army depots to receiving countries.

2. US Army will consider providing drivers to deliver trucks to border of receiving countries where fesible but insist upon delivery of other goods at depots at earliest possible moment. Also unwilling to warehouse and guard goods beyond scheduled departure of troops.

3. We propose to turn over goods to be transported across Europe by rail or truck to receiving governments at army depots. This would make receivers responsible for such overland transportation and pass title of them upon leaving depots. Tremendous saving of accounting responsibility for UNRRA as well as avoidance of setting up complete transportation system.

4. This would involve quick and careful planning on part of governments including transit agreements with occupying armies where involved--recruitment of truck drivers-- arrangements for fueling repair guards etc., and or arrangements for transport by rail. UNRRA would of course assist in all possible ways where such assistance useful.

5. Would hope to secure supplies for Italy, Greece, Jugoslavia and Albania mostly from American bases in Italy, but there is likely to be substantial quantity which receiving country would have chance to obtain in western Europe if prepared to move overland or by sea or a combination of these.

6. Please comment immediately on practicability of such arrangements after consultation with government to which you accredited.

7. Can government undertake responsibility. B. Can they be ready to begin moving goods by late September. C. Comment fully on any problem in this connection which may be peculiar to your country not obvious here.

7. We also intend to discuss proposal paragraph 3 with Washington Representatives of receiving governments here.

8. Arrangements this operation will be under supervision of Karl Borders, Deputy Chief Supply, Headquarters, who is assigned plenary powers to direct whole operation. He will proceed to Paris and Caserta shortly and will issue such instructions to AND such arrangements with Mission as necessary. He will, and Missions should, repeat communications to Headquarters and ERO until further notice.
= Lehman

e 606,
+a

ing
ements
ment
repair
ort
ll
l.

g
by rail
possible wa

Czechoslovak Office for Relief and Rehabilitation,
Department for Motocars :
Dr Steiner.

Information for the Coor...
Czechoslovak Offi...

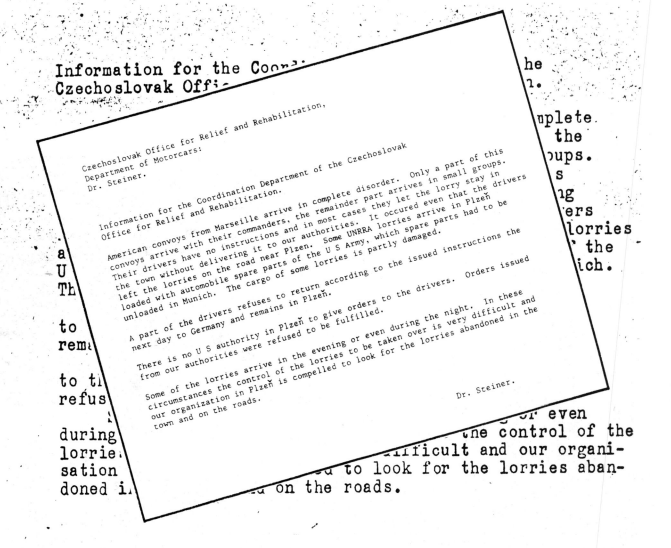

Czechoslovak Office for Relief and Rehabilitation,
Department of Motorcars:
Dr. Steiner.

Information for the Coordination Department of the Czechoslovak
Office for Relief and Rehabilitation.

American convoys from Marseille arrive in complete disorder. Only a part of this
convoys arrive with their commanders, the remainder part arrives in small groups.
Their drivers have no instructions and in most cases they let the lorry stay in
the town without delivering it to our authorities. It occured even that the drivers
left the lorries on the road near Plzen. Some UNRRA lorries arrive in Plzeň
loaded with automobile spare parts of the U S Army, which spare parts had to be
unloaded in Munich. The cargo of some lorries is partly damaged.

A part of the drivers refuses to return according to the issued instructions the
next day to Germany and remains in Plzeň.

There is no U S authority in Plzeň to give orders to the drivers. Orders issued
from our authorities were refused to be fulfilled.

Some of the lorries arrive in the evening or even during the night. In these
circumstances the control of the lorries to be taken over is very difficult and
our organization in Plzeň is compelled to look for the lorries abandoned in the
town and on the roads.

Dr. Steiner.

or even
the control of the
difficult and our organi-
sation to look for the lorries abandoned on the roads.

Dr Steiner.

The UNRRA Motor Transport and Maintenance Branch at 15 Portland Place, London W1, tried to encourage the US Army Transportation Office at 52 Champs-Elysees in Paris to get vehicles out of their SURPROP (Surplus Property) parks at Vincennes, Lerain-Prouvy and Marseilles, and deliver them to Lt Col Davis and Capt Steiner, transport officers at the UNRRA Mission in Praha. They in turn tried to get drivers from Dr Schlesinger at CRR in Praha. Eventually the Czechoslovak Army offered a few hundred drivers who would be sent in cycles by train to western Europe to pick up thousands of vehicles they decided they wanted to acquire. It was all down-hill from there as nothing worked the way it was supposed to.

First, there were complaints about US Army security at the various motor pools in the West. It was very lax and by the end of 1945 many vehicles had been cannibalized for parts. Then, the Czechoslovaks wanted a full compliment of tools, spare parts and 12 jerricans of gasoline with each inspected jeep they picked up. The US Army wanted 17¢ per gallon for all gasoline besides that in the main tank. Ultimately, there were not enough Czechoslovakian drivers so the US Army volunteered drivers to take the vehicles to Pilsen where the Czechoslovak government had set up its receiving depot near the airport.

Add to this situation the fact that the British were trying to reduce the surplus vehicle count in England by shipping them to France and you have a daisy-chain of mega-proportions. Convoys of over 125 vehicles left France without any written knowledge of the contents and when they arrived in Pilsen nobody knew how many they had lost. When someone started counting, the typical official UNRRA *shipped/arrived* convoy figures looked like this: 120/67, 120/84, 981/720, 90/88, 90/83, 1079/742, 92/78, 99/50, 85/75, and 75/44. Convoy 10-46 left Marseilles with 989 2½ ton trucks, 40 jeeps and 1080 trailers and when it arrived in Pilsen a week later it contained 826 2½ ton trucks, 27 jeeps and 821 trailers. Some vehicles got no more than

UNRRA/3821 US surplus becomes the property of the UNRRA at the number 5 quay in Piraeus, Greece.

on preparations made for reception of American vehicles.

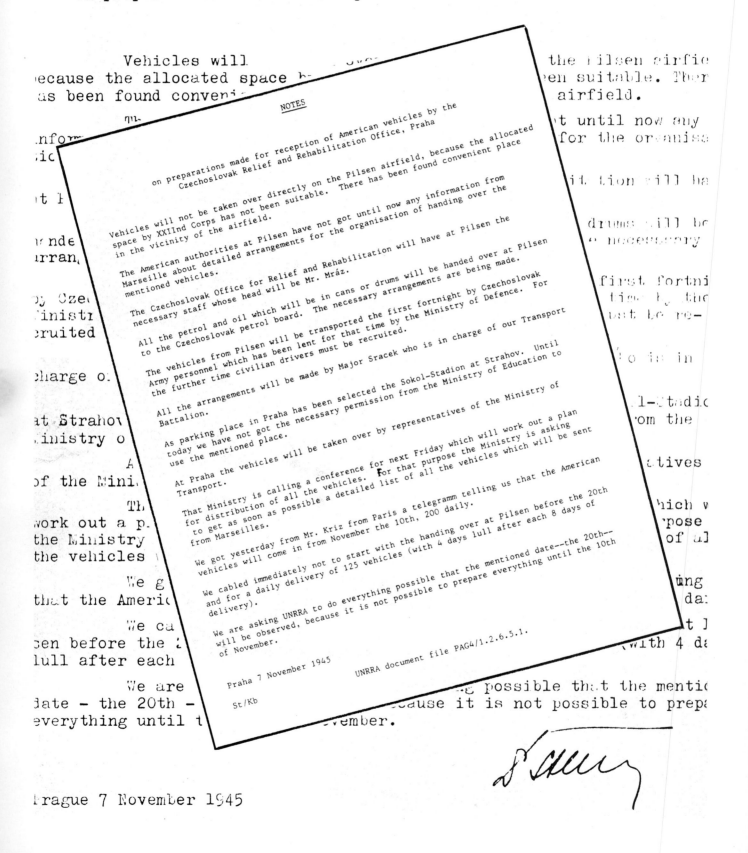

NOTES

on preparations made for reception of American vehicles by the
Czechoslovak Relief and Rehabilitation Office, Praha

Vehicles will not be taken over directly on the Pilsen airfield, because the allocated space by XXIInd Corps has not been suitable. There has been found convenient place in the vicinity of the airfield.

The American authorities at Pilsen have not got until now any information from Marseille about detailed arrangements for the organisation of handing over the mentioned vehicles.

The Czechoslovak Office for Relief and Rehabilitation will have at Pilsen the necessary staff whose head will be Mr. Mráz.

All the petrol and oil which will be in cans or drums will be handed over at Pilsen to the Czechoslovak petrol board. The necessary arrangements are being made.

The vehicles from Pilsen will be transported the first fortnight by Czechoslovak Army personnel which has been lent for that time by the Ministry of Defence. For the further time civilian drivers must be recruited.

All the arrangements will be made by Major Sracek who is in charge of our Transport Battalion.

As parking place in Praha has been selected the Sokol-Stadion at Strahov. Until today we have not got the necessary permission from the Ministry of Education to use the mentioned place.

At Praha the vehicles will be taken over by representatives of the Ministry of Transport.

That Ministry is calling a conference for next Friday which will work out a plan for distribution of all the vehicles. For that purpose the Ministry is asking to get as soon as possible a detailed list of all the vehicles which will be sent from Marseilles.

We got yesterday from Mr. Kriz from Paris a telegramm telling us that the American vehicles will come in from November the 10th, 200 daily.

We cabled immediately not to start with the handing over at Pilsen before the 20th and for a daily delivery of 125 vehicles (with 4 days lull after each 8 days of delivery).

We are asking UNRRA to do everything possible that the mentioned date--the 20th-- will be observed, because it is not possible to prepare everything until the 10th of November.

Praha 7 November 1945

St/Kb

UNRRA document file PAG4/1.2.6.5.1.

Prague 7 November 1945

How many people will a MA hold? Here Jiri Trnka (driving) proves that ten is not too many for his "Dedek" in post-war Czechoslovakia. The two pictures below were taken recently on a farm in Czechoslovakia as yet another MA was saved from destruc-

tion. This one had been used for farming and had the original Go Devil engine replaced with a similar Soviet engine. Thank goodness Lady Bird Johnson never got her rural beautification program started in Czechoslovakia, or this one would have gone to the scrap heap.

Surplus vehicles
CORRECTED COPY

TRUCKS FOR D.P.

General Specifications:

1. All vehicles herewith requested are accepted subject to the mutual understanding that they are in operating condition and will be serviced according to Army standard operating procedure ready for convoy by UNRRA personnel to Holland, Germany or Austria including oiling (crankcase, transmission transfer and differential) greasing and winterizing when temperature conditions require.

2. All vehicles, in so far as the requisite items are available in Ordnance Depots, shall be provided with:

   (a) standard on-vehicle tool kits (wrenches, pliers, hammer, screwdriver, etc.).

   (b) Standard on-vehicle accessories (jack, pump, tire irons, engine crank, grease gun, etc.).

   (c) As many copies as are available of pertinent operating and repair manuals, lubrication check chart and standard nomenclature lists (maintenance and overhaul parts; also "all parts").

   (d) All of the items listed in (a), (b) and (c) above shall be substantially itemized on shipping tickets and transported as cargo with the trucks.

3. Essential equipment to be provided with each truck:

   (a) Spare tire mounted on rim and inflated.

   (b) Tarpaulin and cab cover for vehicles requiring same.

   (c) At least one par of rear tire chains, if available.

   (d) Tow chain and pioneer kit, if available.

4. Shipping tickets for each vehicle shall bear a line item for each vehicle showing:

   (a) Army nomenclature of vehicle

   (b) Make

   (c) Model

   (d) U.S. Army serial number

   (e) Engine number

   (f) Chassis number

5. According to basic agreement between the U.S. Army and UNRRA each truck shall be supplied with 12 cans, safety, 5 gal. (Jerry) filled with gasolene, one filling spout and three gallons motor oil, winter grade SAC-10. This includes jeeps.

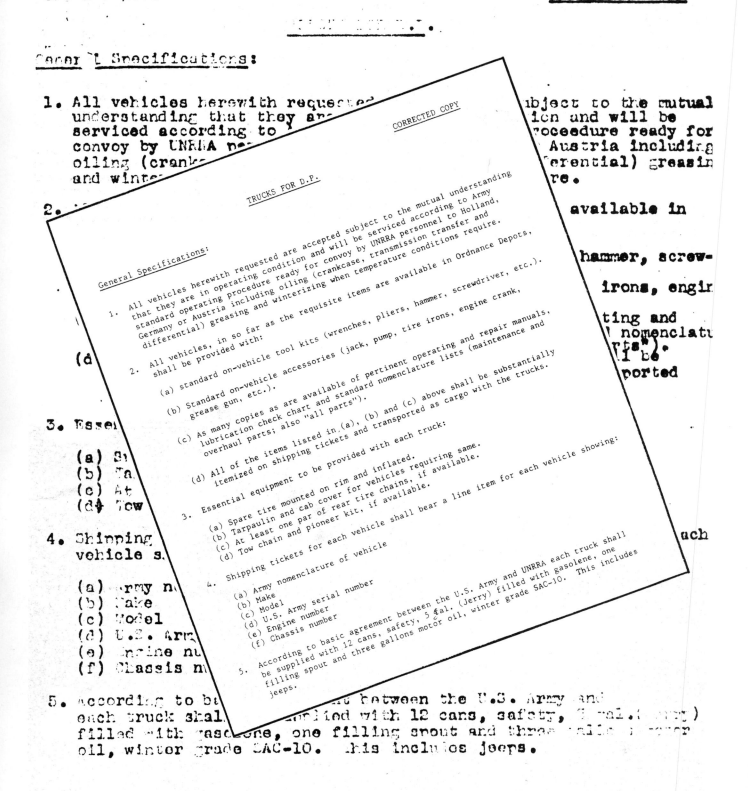

30 km from Marseilles and some returned rather than going on. Many were abandoned or stolen. Some drivers simply "toured Europe" until the vehicles would go no further.

There were still more complaints on the Pilsen end. The motor park there had no guards and no receiving system at the start. Because of the size and disbursement of the convoys they were apt to arrive in Pilsen at any hour, day or night. The Czechoslovaks complained that many US Army convoys arrived in Pilsen loaded with US Property that should have

been dropped off in Munich. The US drivers arrived without officers or orders and *"in most cases"* simply parked their jeeps in Pilsen town and walked away. There was no US Military Authority in Pilsen and the Americans refused to take orders from the Czechoslovaks. They were supposed to return to Germany the day after arrival but some stayed for weeks, or as long as their money lasted.

The road between France and Czechoslovakia was littered with US vehicles. Every office involved was flooding the others with paperwork and complaints about the problem. The blackmarketeers were having a field day. As usual, the Army appointed an Investigation Committee and on 6 May 1946 its chief, a Lt Col Cohen, submitted his report through a man named Gabler in Paris. Cohen had

found 21 trucks at Arolsen near Karlsruhe, Germany. At Frankfurt he found 9 trucks and 19 trailers. At Nürnberg he found 2 trucks and at St Rambert, France he found 8 trucks and 12 trailers. In other places he gathered up 17 trucks, 11 trailers and 2 jeeps which he sent along to an UNRRA assembly point in Metz, France. Of the convoy of 975 trucks, 1070 trailers and 40 jeeps he was tracing, 906 trucks, 887 trailers and 34 jeeps could be accounted for. He was short 69 trucks, 183 trailers and 6 jeeps on *a single* convoy (enough to start a small business).

Based on Cohen's and other recommendations it was decided to split the cost of the losses (jeeps were valued at $502.00 each) between the shipper and the receiver. Convoys were reduced to a maximum of 40 vehicles and empty ve-

UNRRA/3680 Guy Hickok, Director of the Balkan Central Clearing Office in Rome talking to the lead driver of a convoy of US trucks headed for Albania.

UNRRA/3788 A column of jeeps with lady drivers ready to depart Antwerp, Belgium for points East. Notice the unusual guard on the blackout driving lamp of the near jeep and the German or British jerrican on the second one.

All photos with an UNRRA number were kindly supplied by Hartmut Hagner, former Chief of Reference and Sound Archives at the United Nations in New York. When I visited the UN archives first in 1986 I could tell I was the first MV freak ever to examine the photo files. It was almost like the best dream any history buff could have. Tens of thousands of beautifully preserved 4 x 5 negatives of the rarest-of-the-rare, all carefully cataloged and available for inspection. (The documents in the Czechoslovakian section of this book are from the same archive).

During my visits the only other researchers I saw were para-legals looking for documents for use in deportation hearings against former Nazis. There is no doubt that with the publication of this book many others will begin to search the UN files. An enormous amount of MV information awaits the diligent in New York.

The UN Archive is housed in a very ordinary building at 345 Park Avenue, 12th floor in New York City. Hours are Monday through Friday 9:00 - 4:30. You should phone (212) 963-8681 first to make sure you can access what you want on the day you intend to visit. The staff is small for such an important archive.

hicles were interspersed with loaded ones to pick up the loads of any that became disabled. Convoy Commanders began signing for all convoy contents and a proper receiving was made in Pilsen where 150 German POWs were assigned to marshalling activities inside a fenced and guarded compound. Arrangements were made with the Skoda automobile factory in Pilsen and the firm of Csl Zbrojovka in Brno to repair all the vehicles arriving in damaged condition. In addition the Czechoslovaks asked that vehicles be delivered in maximum quantities of 125 per day for 8 days running and then a lull of 4 days before starting another 8 day cycle. Any spare fuel in vehicles arriving in Pilsen was taken over by the Czechoslovak Office for Mineral Oils and just enough fuel was left in vehicles to get them to their next destination.

From that point onward things worked considerably better and most of the later problems related to the condition of the vehicles arriving in Czechoslovakia. An extremely interesting example can be found in a shipment of 108 MAs unloaded from the *SS Ritchie* in Trieste, Italy on 30 March 1946. They were sent directly to Csl Zbrojovka in Brno for decrating and assembly. Of the 108 jeeps, exactly half required 2nd and/or 3rd eschelon repairs to make them ready for use. The Csl Zbrojovka repair record on this shipment is as follows:

Record of additional repairs on vehicles Jeep, delivered to Czechoslovakia in cases, performed by Csl Zbrojovka, Brno.

Except of normal work (i.e. assemblying and testing of the vehicles) following additional repairs had to be carried out. We ask for your approval as to the repairs, so that we could put the additional work expences on account.

Serial No:	Engine No:
Description of work:	

78.659   78.721
Removal, straightening and assembly of steering rods, and steering adjusting.

78.664   78.548
Dismantling, cleaning and assembly of brake master cylinder. Adjusting and bleeding of brakes.

78.486   7.849
Removal of gear-levers and exhaust pipe, adjusting, straightening and assembly.

78.824   78.854
Removal and assembly of front L.H. wheel, brake shoes and brake wheel cylinder. Adjusting of brakes/drag remedy/.

UNRRA/4324 Motorcycles may look out of place in a book on jeeps but this was too pretty to omit. A surplus lot goes to the UNRRA in Greece.

SOROKIN
duplicate

from Dr.B.Steiner.

aut 2842/46

UNRRA Mission for Czechoslovakia,
att.Ing.V.Sorokin,

P r a g u e ,X.,
Palace Atlas.

Re:Additional repairs on Jeeps from Trieste.

Dear Sir:

On March the 3oth,1946 the SS Albert Ritchie
unloaded for us in Trieste a consignement of 108 vehicles
JEEP,packed in boxes.

The firm Čsl.Zbrojovka in Brno was entrusted with
the re-assembly of the 108 vehicles.Enclosed we are forwar-
ding to you a translated copy of their report of repairs
performed.The report states that in 54 cases additional
repairs had to be performed,which are 2nd and 3rd echelon
work.It can be said that because of the bad technical
condition of these vehicles,their lifetime will be shorter
that exspected as well as their workingcapacity.Also the
assembling costs will be much higher than calculated.

We would be very glad indeed if you could take
action in order to find a way of recompensation.

Sincerely yours:

Czechoslovak Office for
Relief and Rehabilitation.

A photocopy of an original document in the archives of the UN in New York. When I found this letter dealing with "108 vehicles JEEP, packed in boxes", I knew I had started to crack the mystery of all the MAs in Czechoslovakia.

1 enclosure

Prague,September 11th,1946.

Un.R.

1 2 IX. 1946.

174

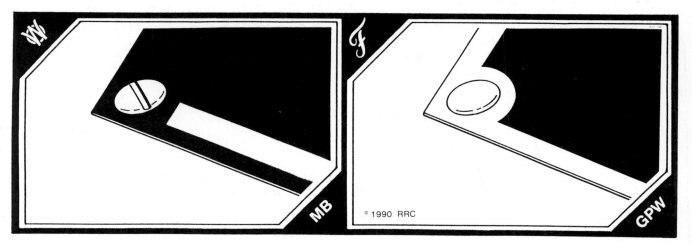

© 1990 RRC

Data plates of steel, brass, zinc and probably other materials as well can be found on old MBs and GPWs. There are at least a dozen different variations of the copy found on them, not to mention foreign language plates like Chinese and Russian. Another interesting difference between Ford and Willys is depicted above. Ford riveted their data plates to the glove box door on jeeps while Willys-Overland used bolts and nuts to hold them in place. I have seen data plates with only the month and year stamped on them, but no day of delivery.

78.634   282.265
Dismantling, cleaning and assembly of clutch. Adjusting of transfer case shifting mechanism/would not shift/.

79.610   79.092
Removal, cleaning and assembly of wheels, drums, brakes adjusting and brake-fluid refilling.

85.508   85.509
Removal of exhaust repairing the flexible hose, exhaust and brake pipe transfer, shortening the clutch rod and welding the bolt to bracket.

78.599   79.517
Clutch and gear shift adjusting, shifting resistence remedy, shortening of clutch control rod, removal repair and assembly of fuel pump, removal of rear wheels and brake wheel cylinders and remedy of dragging.

79.431   78.807
Rear wheels, brakes and wheel cylinders removal, remedy of dragging and shortening of clutch contr. rod.

79.020   70.059
Clutch repair and adjusting, straightening of clutch controls and gear-shift mechanism adjusting.

78.673   78.729
Remedy of steering joints play, dismantling, cleaning and adjusting of hand-brake.

79.492   79.501
Repair of body above rear R.H. wheel/drags on brake drum/.

78.682   79.475
Removal and assembly of front wheels and brakes/dragging and scraping remedy/.

79.246   162.549
Removal, repair and assembly of petrol tank. Steering joints play remedy.

79.281   79.291
Dismantling, repair and assembly of master cylinder, brakes cleaning and adjusting, brake fluid refill, starter and wiring repair.

79.554   79.512
Gear lever welding, shift mechanism adjusting.

79.048   80.044
Radiator repair and welding of engine shield.

79.333   79.353
Removal, repair and assembly of radiator.

78.676   78.690
Removal, repair and assembly of radiator.

79.377   79.387
Removal, repair and assembly of radiator.

78.580   78.595
Gear shift lever welding, ignition and carburetor repair.

78.829   92.099
Radiator repair, gear shift lever welding, removal, straightening, adjusting and assembly of gear shift mechanism.

79.406   79.132
Gear shift lever welding, fitting and adjusting of gear shift mechanism and bleeding rear brakes.

79.351   79.367
Removal, welding and assembly of gear shift lever, gear shift mechanism adjusting, clutch adjusting and clutch contr. rod shortening.

79.168   80.109
Brake drum regrinding, removal and assembly of brake drums, cleaning of shoes.

79.428   79.443
Removal, repair and assembly of radiator.

78.442   79.511
Removal, repair and assembly of radiator.

79.327   79.292
Removal, repair and assembly of petrol tank, welding a screw M6, gear-lever welding and gear shift mechanism adjusting.

79.449   79.460
Removal, repair and assembly of radiator, valve tappets adjusting, brake hose repair.

79.027   85.552
Radiator removal, repair and assembly.

79.400   79.360
Radiator removal, repair and assembly, exhaust repair and lighting system repair.

79.741   80.081
Radiator removal, repair and assembly.

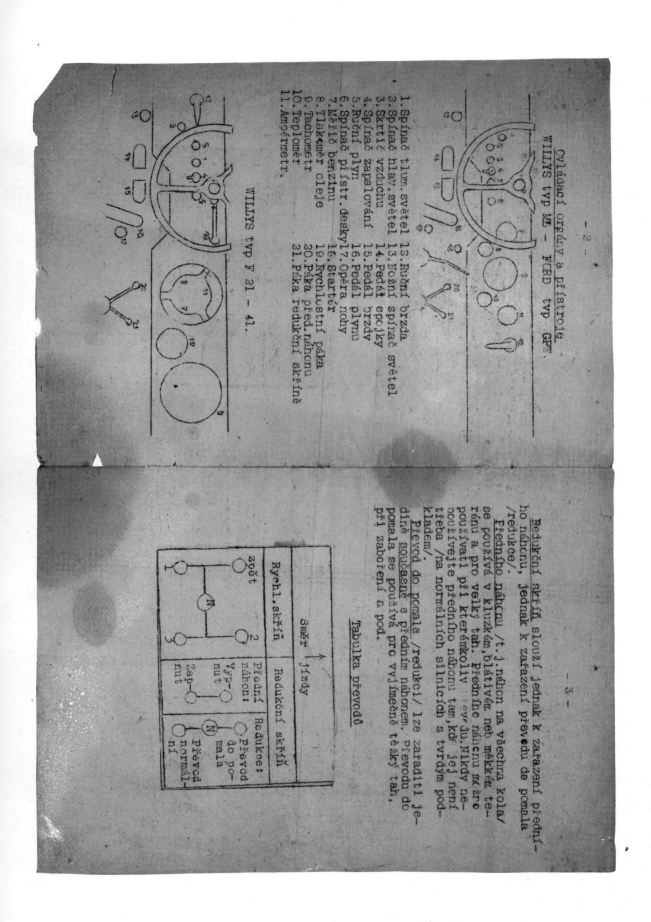

Ovládací orgány a přístroje

WILLYS typ MB - FORD typ GPW

1. Spínač tlum. světel
2. Spínač hlav. světel
3. Škrtíč vzduchu
4. Spínač zapalování
5. Ruční plyn
6. Spínač přístr. desky
7. Měřič benzinu
8. Tlakoměr oleje
9. Tachometr
10. Teploměr
11. Ampérmetr.

12. Ruční brzda
13. Nožní spínač světel
14. Pedál spojky
15. Pedál brzdy
16. Pedál plynu
17. Opěra nohy
18. Startér
19. Rychlostní páka
20. Páka před. náhonu
21. Páka redukční skříně

WILLYS typ F 31 - 41.

Redukční skříň slouží jednak k zařazení předního náhonu, jednak k zařazení převodu do pomala
/redukce/.

Předního náhonu /t.j. náhon na všechna kola/
se používá v kluzkém, blátivém neb měkkém te-
rénu a pro velký tah. Předního náhonu nc zro
používati při kterémkoliv převodu. Nikdy ne-
používejte předního náhonu tam, kde jej není
třeba /na normálních silnicích s tvrdým pod-
kladem/.

Převod do pomala /redukci/ lze zařaditi je-
diné současně s předním náhonem. Převodu do
pomala se používá pro vyjímečně těžký tah,
při zaboření a pod.

Tabulka převodů

Směr jízdy →	Rychl.skříň	Redukční skříň	
		Přední náhon:	Redukce:
	zpět		
	1	vyp-nut	do po-mala
	2		
	3	zap-nut	Převod normál-ní

Pages 2 and 3 of the drivers manual supplied to Jiri Trnka along with the MA he purchased from the UNRRA for $755.00.

78.581   78.605
Radiator removal, repair and assembly, front mudguard welding and steering adjusting.

78.729   92.465
Radiator removal, repair and assembly.

78.584   70.543
Radiator removal, repair and assembly.

79.569   79.738
Radiator removal, repair and assembly.

79.397   79.408
Brake pedal and shaft repair.

79.292   79.315
Radiator removal, repair and assembly.

79.901   92.414
Securing bolt welding, repair of 2 keys, grinding 4 washers of gear shift mechanism and universal joint repair.

79.230   79.264
Battery box repair and 1 tyre repair.

79.813   79.823
Burst cyl. block repair, valve grinding, making a bolt for oil pump housing, piston rings repair, countershaft exchange, oil pipe exchange, making 1 gasket-head cylinder, steering gear cover exchange, tyres and tubes repair.

79.435   101.177
Master cylinder repair, brakes cleaning and adjusting, brake fluid refilling.

78.460   187.312
Removal, repair and assembly of brakes/ drag remedy/.

79.179   78.788
Repair and fastening of exhaust, shift mechanism adjusting, steering adjusting, steering box cover exchange.

78.762   78.597
Starting motor repair, removal front R.H. wheel, shoes, cylinder brake assembly, drag remedy, fluid exchange and brakes bleeding.

79.121   92.489
Valve seats regrinding, valve grinding, big-end bearings scraping, front bumper repair, engine adjusting and testing.

78.783   78.841
Brakes repair/rear L.H. wheel drag remedy/.

79.381   79.790
Valve seats regrinding, making 1 cylinder head gasket, removal of conn. rods and pistons, rust removal, valve grinding and adjusting, fan pulley exchange, throttle, pedal and exhaust valve dragging remedy.

79.258   79.260
Gear lever welding, rear shift mechanism adjusting, removal, repair of master cylinder and brake hose, brakes bleeding, valve clearance, adusting, 4 valve spring exchange, making 1 cyl. head gasket, first speed shifting bracket exchange and synchronising collar exchange.

78.616   GPW7583
Exhaust pipe welding, making 1 cyl. head gasket, valve clearance adjusting, making 2 valve spring retainers, brakes bleeding and adjusting. Lights, horn and carburetor repair, removal and repair of transfer reduction.

79.153   79.159
Master cylinder and brake pedal removal and repair, brake fluid exchange, brakes bleeding and adjusting, generator repair/ noisy/, el. horn exchange.

79.726   79.735
Valve clearance adjusting, 3 valve springs exchange, throttle pedal deficient, gear shift mechanism adjusting, hand-brake drag remedy, shoes repair and brake pedal rebushing.

78.725   104,214
Making 1 cyl. head gasket, removal of rust from engine, valve clearance adjusting, 4 springs exchange, big-end bearings fitting, valves grinding, exhaust pipe-valve

A sergeant with the US 103rd Infantry Division checks the papers of Austrian civilians in Innsbruck on 23 May 1945. The unusual tires on the jeep may have made it a little quieter on the highway.

dragging remedy, front bumper repair, throttle pedal exchange, thread cutting on 3 bolts, 3 bolts adding.

78.720　　　78.760
Valve grinding and clearance adjusting, retainers exchange and radiator repair.

79.385　　　79.393
Radiator repair, clutch adjusting and clutch control cable shortening.

78.586　　　92.458
Radiator removal, repair and assembly.

78.658　　　92.400
Removal or radiator, front bumper re-bushing of hole for distributor/cyl. block burst 70 mm/, valve clearance adjusting, starter repair, brake hose exchange, repair and cleaning of the whole pressure lubricating system/water removal/, exhaust manifold gasket and water pump gasket making, gear shift mechanism adjusting, radiator repair and fan belt adjusting.

78.728　　　79.939
Valve grinding and clearance adjusting, making 1 gasket for exhaust manifold, gear shift mechanism adjustment, rear L.H. wheel repair/drag remedy/.

78.490　　　80.034
Brake fluid exchange, hydraulic brake system cleaning, brakes bleeding, brake shoes and drums cleaning and shifting mechanism adjusting.

79.823　　　78.866
Tyre repair.

END OF REPORT

Editor's Note: Certainly this report leaves at least a few questions in the mind of the reader. It specifically states that these jeeps were delivered from Trieste to Brno "in cases" but the GPW and MB engine numbers would seem to indicate that *some* of these jeeps were not new and were probably uncrated when received in Brno.

On the other hand, it is extremely interesting to note that most of these MAs had an engine number within about 50 numbers of the frame serial number. The diction, spelling, placement of punctuation, etc., in this report is faithful to the original.

Major General McBride, commander of 3rd Army's 80th Infantry Division arrives at his new command post in Braunau, Austria (Hitler's birthplace) on 5 May 1945. McBride's jeep was a highly modified version of the original, having armor, mudflaps, custom made fenders and plenty of firepower.

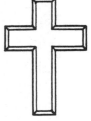

There were over 8000 Chaplains serving with the US Armed Services at the high point during WWII. Here a "Holy Joe" with the 253rd Infantry Regiment of the 63rd Division climbs into his jeep for a tour to the front in France in February 1945.

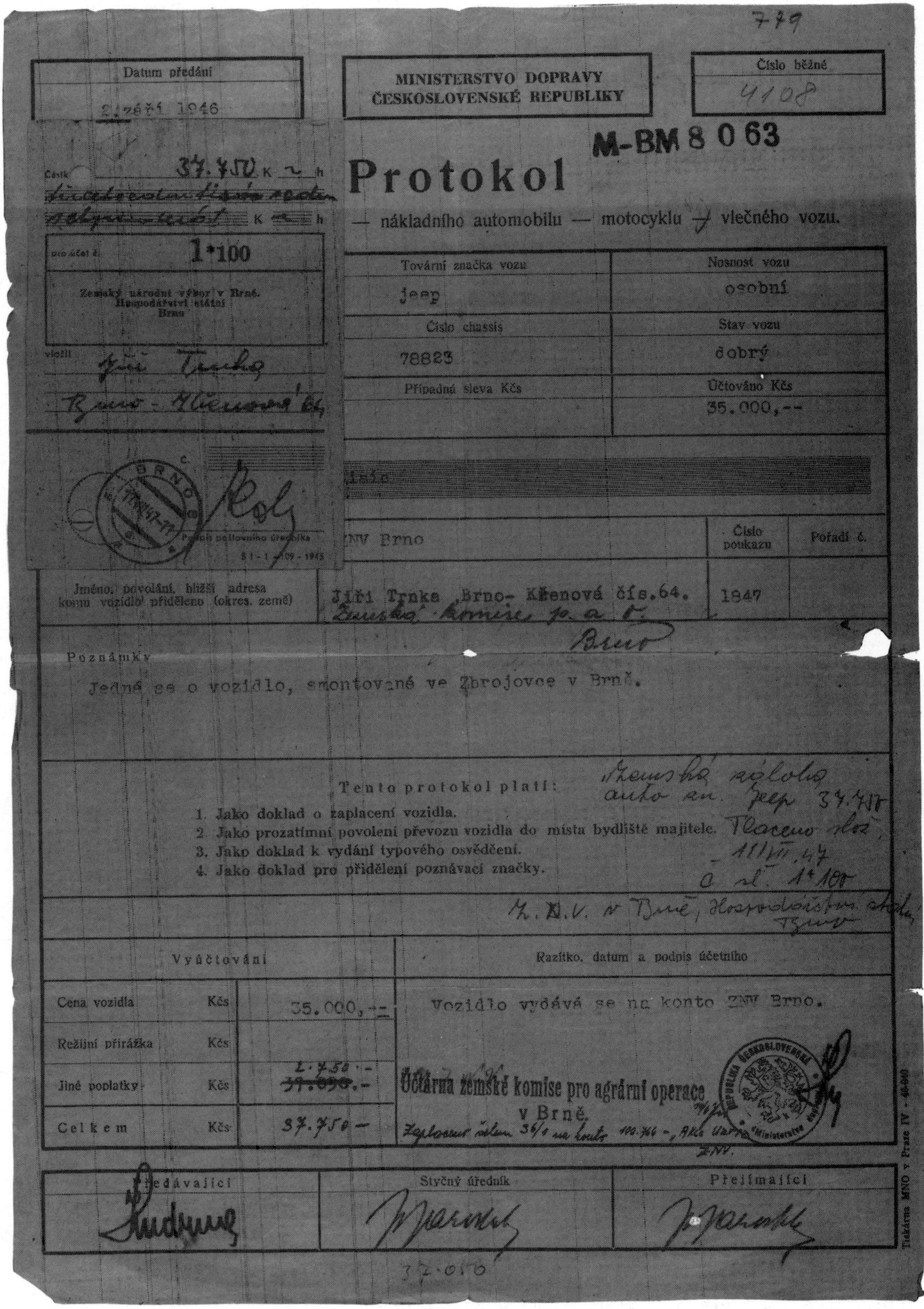

Datum předání	MINISTERSTVO DOPRAVY ČESKOSLOVENSKÉ REPUBLIKY	Číslo běžné
S.září 1946		4108

M-BM 8 0 63

Protokol

— nákladního automobilu — motocyklu — vlečného vozu.

Čásk 37.750 K ~ h

~~~~~~~~~~~~~~~~~~~~ K ~ h

1·100

Zemský národní výbor v Brně.
Hospodářství státní
Brno

vozil Jiří Trnka
Brno – Křenová 64,

Tovární značka vozu	Nosnost vozu
jeep	osobní
Číslo chassis	Stav vozu
78823	dobrý
Případná sleva Kčs	Účtováno Kčs
	35.000,--

		Číslo poukazu	Pořadí č.
ZNV Brno			
Jméno, povolání, bližší adresa komu vozidlo přiděleno (okres, země)	Jiří Trnka ,Brno- Křenová čís.64. Zemská komise p. a. o. Brno	1847	

Poznámky

Jedná se o vozidlo, smontované ve Zbrojovce v Brně.

Tento protokol platí:

1. Jako doklad o zaplacení vozidla.
2. Jako prozatímní povolení převozu vozidla do místa bydliště majitele.
3. Jako doklad k vydání typového osvědčení.
4. Jako doklad pro přidělení poznávací značky.

Zemská záloha auto an jeep 37.417 Placeno dle 11/III 47 o č. 1·100

Z. N. V. v Brně, Hospodářství státní Brno

Vyúčtování			Razítko, datum a podpis účetního
Cena vozidla	Kčs	35.000,--	Vozidlo vydává se na konto ZNV Brno.
Režijní přirážka	Kčs		
Jiné poplatky	Kčs	2.750 --	Účtárna zemské komise pro agrární operace v Brně,
Celkem	Kčs	37.750 --	

Předávající	Styčný úředník	Přejímající

A copy of the report from the Czechoslovak Ministry of Transport recording the important data about Jiri Trnka's MA at the time he bought it. The letters in the license plate number (M-BM) stand for: M - State of Moravia, BM - City of Brno.

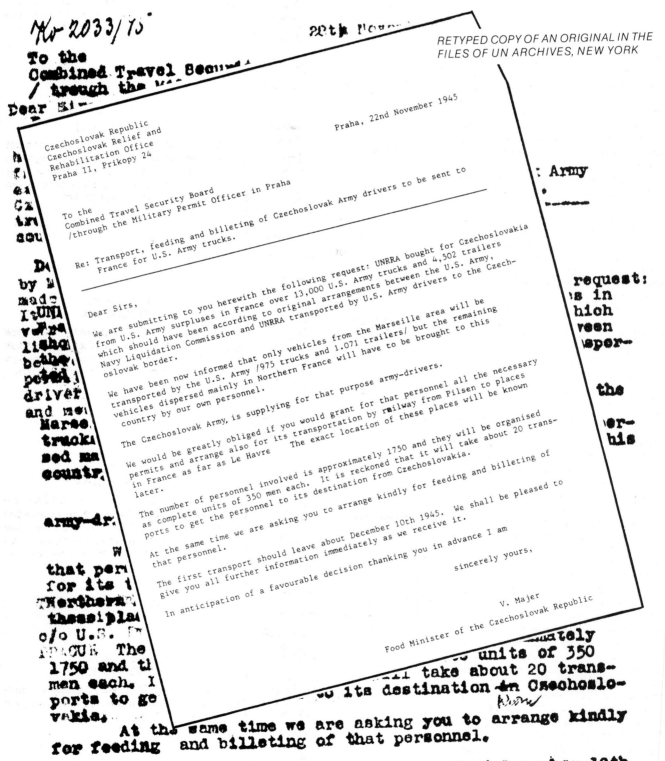

Czechoslovak Republic
Czechoslovak Relief and
Rehabilitation Office
Praha II, Prikopy 24

Praha, 22nd November 1945

To the
Combined Travel Security Board
/through the Military Permit Officer in Praha

Re: Transport, feeding and billeting of Czechoslovak Army drivers to be sent to
France for U.S. Army trucks.

Dear Sirs,

We are submitting to you herewith the following request: UNRRA bought for Czechoslovakia
from U.S. Army surpluses in France over 13,000 U.S. Army trucks and 4,502 trailers
which should have been according to original arrangements between the U.S. Army,
Navy Liquidation Commission and UNRRA transported by U.S. Army drivers to the Czechoslovak border.

We have been now informed that only vehicles from the Marseille area will be
transported by the U.S. Army /975 trucks and 1.071 trailers/ but the remaining
vehicles dispersed mainly in Northern France will have to be brought to this
country by our own personnel.

The Czechoslovak Army, is supplying for that purpose army-drivers.

We would be greatly obliged if you would grant for that personnel all the necessary
permits and arrange also for its transportation by railway from Pilsen to places
in France as far as Le Havre   The exact location of these places will be known
later.

The number of personnel involved is approximately 1750 and they will be organised
as complete units of 350 men each. It is reckoned that it will take about 20 trans-
ports to get the personnel to its destination from Czechoslovakia.

At the same time we are asking you to arrange kindly for feeding and billeting of
that personnel.

The first transport should leave about December 10th 1945. We shall be pleased to
give you all further information immediately as we receive it.

In anticipation of a favourable decision thanking you in advance I am

sincerely yours,

V. Majer

Food Minister of the Czechoslovak Republic

MB/GPW VINTAGE

CAUTION: all lists of this type must be considered approximate. Draw no conclusions from any single source.

The value of being able to identify what you have within the range of what was manufactured is of paramount importance to collectors of any rarity, be it a coin, a jeep or other collectible. Much of this book is an effort to more clearly define the many small nuances of production that make one jeep different from another.

As no clear universal definition exists as to the sub-species of jeeps produced during WWII, I have decided against the advice of experts to attempt to categorize jeeps of the period into 6 distinct groups. Naturally, there is some overlapping and perhaps someone else can come up with a system that makes more sense. While we wait for a better system I will proffer the one that follows.

The AAW system is an attempt to separate production of MBs and GPWs at points in the serial numbering and dates of delivery by certain features that *originally* were common to one group or another. Such a system should be helpful to restorers who wish to return a vehicle to the condition it was in when it left the factory. It should also help anyone who is looking at a vehicle with intent to acquire it. If you know what general features a certain vehicle should have, it will be helpful in assessing the cost and difficulty of truly restoring it. Because of the soaring value of certain sub-species within WWII jeep production it is well worth knowing which sub-specie you are dealing with.

Following the classification system is the largest list of serial numbers and dates of delivery for MBs and GPWs ever published, as well as other relevant information. I am grateful to all who responded to our call for serial number and date of delivery information in volume I of this book, especially Darcy Miller. I repeat the call here. If you have a jeep or know of one with a serial number and date of delivery NOT shown on this list, or if you can correct any error in the list, please do so. In the Americas send numbers to: MB/GPW List, Box 810, Lakeville, MN 55044-0810 USA. In Europe send them to : Seven Winds, Farningham Hill Road, Farningham, Kent, England. In the Pacific send them to 91-93 Market St., Smithfield, NSW, Australia.

MB S/Ns	GPW S/Ns		
100000	?	NOV '41	PROTOTYPES

TYPICAL FEATURES

V E P — 7% of production

| 120700 | 16000 | MAY '42 |
| 143507 | 20000 | |

VERY EARLY PRODUCTION

No glove box door, round muffler, AC air filter, rubber hood bumpers, solid wheels, 2 hinges on tool box lid, 3 bolt spare tire carrier, no blackout driving lamp, makers name on rear panel, slat grill on Willys.

E P — 7% of production

| 158372 | 45000 | AUG '42 |
| 174739 | 60000 | |

EARLY PRODUCTION

Oakes air filter, oval muffler, combat wheels, locking glove box, keyed ignition switch, 9 slot stamped grill, torque reaction spring, no spare gas can bracket, no trailer light connecting socket.

M S P — 64% of production

| 277000 | 158000 | NOV '43 |
| 284000 | 165000 | |

MID-SERIES PRODUCTION

Blackout driving lamp, wide-mouth gas tank, trailer lighting socket, pintle hook eyes, toggle ignition switch, push-button glove box lock, wooden hood bumpers.

L P — 22% of production

| 445000 | 265000 | AUG '45 |
| 461341 | 278500 | |

LATE PRODUCTION

Composite body, first aid kit, spare tire support bracket, 2 bolt tire carrier, gas can bracket, heavier springs, radio terminal box, no filterette, universal weapon carrier on windshield, fuel filter in gas tank.

▲ WWII PRODUCTION ▲

P W P

POST-WAR PRODUCTION

Civilian jeeps (CJs) with 7 slot grill, headlight trim rings, tail gate, column shift, seat springs, PTO, etc.

WWII ERA JEEP GRILLS

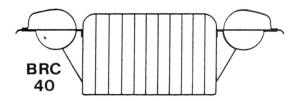

BRC 40

Starting 31 March 1941, 1175 units produced in the S/N range of 2613 to 3650. Supplemental order for 1430 units in the S/N range of 2563 to 2612 for a total of 2675 units. USA registration numbers W-203-0494 to W-2031515 and W-2039179 to W-2039228.

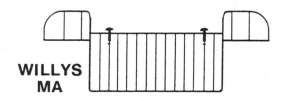

WILLYS MA

Starting 07 June 1941, 1505 units produced in the S/N range of 78401 to 79906 and a second production run of 50 units in the S/N range of 85501 to 85551 for a total of 1555 units*. USA registration numbers W-2018932 to W-2020431.

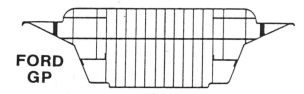

FORD GP

Starting 08 February 1941, 5756 units produced in two series in the S/N ranges of 8500 to 9999 and 14000 to about 16650. USA registration numbers W-2017422 to 2018921, W-2029494 to W-2030493, W-234075 to W-234124 and W-2054778 to W-2069777**

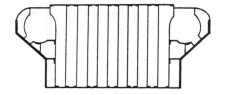

WILLYS MB

FORD GPW

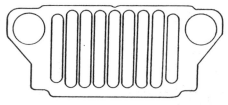

WILLYS "SLAT GRILL"

Starting November 1941, 25808 units produced in the S/N range of 100001 to 125809. USA registration numbers W-2031575 to W-2047574, W-2047614 to 2050213 and 2078697 to 2083803.

WWII STANDARD

FORD GPW

Starting November 1941, 276614 units produced in total in the S/N range of under 500 to about 278500**.

WILLYS MB

Starting March 1942, 335531 units produced in total in the S/N range of 125810 to 461341.

*The source of the MA production numbers is Paul Lafferty, production chief at Willys-Overland from 1940 to 1945.

** Very major problems are encountered in any careful examination of Ford GP production figures. All the figures you have seen are guesses and the ones above are too. Based on known serial numbers (those still in service) one could say that *at least* 3907 GPs were made. Production contracts at Ford Motor Company account for 3700 although these are acknowledged to NOT include special orders. The Ford recap of shipping figures totals 4000. In the LeCroix file at the Henry Ford Museum in Dearborn, Michigan, there is a very interesting document that gives yet another figure that is hard to discount. The document is captioned PRODUCTION OF JEEPS BY MONTHS and gives a figure for each month from February 1941 through July 1945 except the months of March-December 1942. Interestingly the total of GPs *and* GPWs is 277,896, a figure usually cited as the production of GPWs alone. According to this list there were 5756 GPs made. LeCroix was the historian at Ford Motor Company during WWII.

➤

GIs from the 278th Signal Pigeon Company of the 2nd Armored Division are seen releasing carrier pigeons at Magdeburg, Germany on 20 April 1945. The wire cutter and its braces at the front of the jeep were a common and practical improvement for the speedy little ¼ tons.

PRODUCTION OF JEEPS BY MONTHS

	Jan.	Feb.	March	April	May	June	July	Aug.	Sept.	Oct.	Nov.	Dec.
GP 1941		71	653	418	377	292	0	465	1021	1014	1454	0
GP 1942	2											
GPW 1942	77	2118	8920	11159	8924	10762	10395	8801	7688	7208	6068	7260
GPW 1943	5327	5014	5511	5937	8249	6025	6743	7422	7852	7800	7225	7536
GPW 1944	7460	7540	5994	5550	5994	5772	5772	5994	5772	5955	5879	5715
GPW 1945	6041	5416	5936	5202	4295	4069	3514					

Ford Lecroix File

GRAND TOTAL - 277,896

Unit Hours on GPW for the year 1944

97.83	99.35	94.51	87.86	86.80	87.59	87.62	85.10	84.46	84.03	82.18	82.20

"Some Ford Facts . . .", a supplement to Ford advertising published after WWII says very specifically that Ford made "282,381 jeeps" from 1940 to the end of the war. They got that number somewhere and if we (a) assume it is reliable and (b) assume that the chart above is reliable at least as far as GPs are concerned, it would follow that Ford made 276,614 GPWs during the course of production.

WILLYS-OVERLAND SERIAL NUMBER AND DATE OF DELIVERY LIST

100212	NOV	18	1941	110755	JAN	15	1942	128358	MAR	25	1942	174308	SEP	15	1942
100513	NOV	26	1941	111532	JAN	13	1942	130423	MAR	26	1942	175694	SEP	23	1942
100965	NOV	27	1941	111755	JAN	15	1942	130677	MAR	26	1942	176331	SEP	22	1942
101145	NOV	27	1941	111990	JAN	19	1942	130731	MAR	25	1942	177440	SEP	28	1942
101610	DEC	01	1941	112196	JAN	06	1942	130746	MAR	26	1942	182609	OCT	19	1942
102157	DEC	04	1941	112219	JAN	15	1942	130905	MAR	25	1942	188344	NOV	11	1942
102393	DEC	04	1941	112815	JAN	16	1942	130912	MAR	26	1942	188924	NOV	13	1942
102460	DEC	04	1941	113097	JAN	19	1942	131207	MAR	27	1942	194298	DEC	08	1942
102554	DEC	31	1941	113801	JAN	21	1942	131594	MAR	27	1942	194523	DEC	10	1942
103331	DEC	11	1941	113849	JAN	28	1942	132030	MAR	31	1942	196561	DEC	17	1942
103357	DEC	15	1941	115092	JAN	29	1942	132240	MAR	31	1942	196949	DEC	18	1942
103616	DEC	16	1941	115113	JAN		1942	132284	MAR	31	1942	198413	DEC	24	1942
103768	DEC	12	1941	115262	JAN	30	1942	135320	APR	15	1942	200888	JAN	07	1943
103900	DEC	15	1941	115878	FEB	02	1942	135610	JUN	09	1942	200915	JAN	06	1943
104028	DEC	15	1941	115934	FEB	02	1942	139892	MAR	01	1942	201878	NOV	01	1942
104065	DEC	15	1941	117027	FEB	03	1942	140715	JUL	24	1942	201961	JUN	10	1943
104589	DEC	17	1941	117085	FEB	05	1942	145097	MAR	22	1942	204065	JAN	19	1943
104664	DEC	17	1941	118768	FEB	12	1942	146071	MAY	26	1942	208386	FEB	02	1943
105018	DEC	12	1941	119367	FEB	03	1942	147797	JUN	02	1942	208392	FEB	02	1943
105312	DEC	22	1941	119514	FEB	13	1942	147846	JUN	02	1942	211336	FEB	12	1943
105440	DEC	24	1941	119935	FEB	16	1942	148162	JUN	03	1942	213785	FEB	25	1943
106148	DEC	26	1941	120264	FEB	20	1942	148396	JUL	16	1942	215192	FEB	25	1943
106188	DEC	23	1941	120475	APR	29	1942	149817	JUN	09	1942	216868	FEB		1943
106375	DEC	23	1941	121000	MAR	04	1942	152119	JUN	18	1942	218383	MAR	15	1943
107034	DEC	28	1941	121060	FEB	26	1942	153260	JUN	23	1942	221700	MAR	23	1943
107195	DEC	16	1941	121592	FEB	23	1942	153355	JUN	23	1942	227590	APR	14	1943
107507	JAN	20	1942	122112	FEB	24	1942	156198	JUL	03	1942	227770	APR	19	1943
108171	DEC	31	1941	124393	MAR	04	1942	157361	JUL	08	1942	227876	APR	19	1943
109922	JAN	01	1942	125731	MAR	06	1942	160665	JUL	21	1942	228692	APR	21	1943
110153	JAN	08	1942	127130	JUN	12	1942	171238	SEP	02	1942	230534	MAY	03	1943
110702	JAN	14	1942	127955	MAR	16	1942	171418	SEP	02	1942	231423	APR	30	1943

MB

▲ Slat Grill ▲

231500 MAR 03 1943	317925 MAR 28 1944	373566 SEP 22 1944	430149 MAR 27 1945
232625 MAR 03 1943	318924 MAR 31 1944	373596 SEP 22 1944	430650 MAR 28 1945
236792 MAR 23 1943	319494 APR 06 1944	375223 SEP 28 1944	431844 APR 03 1945
237041 MAR 1943	324957 APR 25 1944	376347 OCT 02 1944	432234 APR 04 1945
237486 MAR 26 1943	326015 APR 27 1944	381617 OCT 17 1944	432313 APR 04 1945
237566 MAR 24 1943	328479 MAY 11 1944	382158 OCT 26 1944	432385 APR 04 1945
238249 JUN 02 1943	331964 MAY 12 1944	387168 NOV 22 1944	432474 APR 04 1945
257320 AUG 18 1943	334501 MAY 25 1944	387287 NOV 10 1944	434099 APR 10 1945
260184 AUG 30 1943	337587 JUN 03 1944	388781 NOV 16 1944	435397 MAR 13 1945
261095 SEP 23 1943	339382 JUN 05 1944	393765 DEC 02 1944	436121 APR 23 1945
267086 SEP 25 1943	339841 JUN 07 1944	394263 DEC 05 1944	436332 APR 21 1945
269692 OCT 04 1943	340853 JUN 09 1944	396984 DEC 18 1944	436653 MAR 28 1945
270009 OCT 05 1943	341144 JUN 09 1944	397903 DEC 18 1944	438661 MAY 08 1945
272093 OCT 11 1943	342161 JUN 16 1944	398965 DEC 14 1944	440704 MAR 10 1945
273139 OCT 11 1943	344137 JUN 20 1944	399183 DEC 12 1944	448001 JUN 14 1945
273469 OCT 16 1943	344848 JUN 21 1944	399183 DEC 19 1944	448001 JUN 04 1945
279046 MAR 16 1943	348071 JUL 08 1944	400767 DEC 24 1945	451533 JUN 29 1945
282853 NOV 20 1943	348781 JUL 08 1944	401294 DEC 21 1944	454924 JUL 25 1945
285881 DEC 02 1943	351115 JUL 15 1944	402774 JAN 03 1945	459120 SEP 11 1945
287065 DEC 08 1943	351129 JUL 15 1944	408432 JAN 19 1945	459824 SEP 21 1945
288687 DEC 13 1943	351903 JUL 1944	411202 JAN 29 1945	
293232 DEC 31 1943	352432 JUL 19 1944	411905 JAN 30 1945	
293846 JAN 05 1944	353117 JUL 22 1944	412935 FEB 01 1945	
294440 JAN 05 1944	356083 JUL 31 1944	414570 FEB 07 1945	
296219 JAN 10 1944	356577 AUG 03 1944	415639 MAR 12 1945	
298506 JAN 18 1944	359104 AUG 09 1944	421759 MAR 04 1945	
299533 JAN 18 1944	360098 AUG 11 1944	422795 MAR 04 1945	
302902 FEB 02 1944	360244 AUG 11 1944	423194 MAR 06 1945	
303667 FEB 04 1944	361649 SEP 28 1944	424105 MAR 1945	
304911 FEB 10 1944	367194 SEP 02 1944	425193 MAR 12 1945	
310734 MAR 03 1944	372753 SEP 20 1944	425993 MAR 14 1945	
312114 MAR 08 1944	372771 SEP 23 1944	426498 MAR 16 1945	
313723 MAR 16 1944	372877 SEP 22 1944	427332 MAR 19 1945	
314284 MAR 16 1944	373076 SEP 21 1944	428695 MAR 23 1945	

MB MB MB MB

NOTES, ADDITIONS, CORRECTIONS

FORD MOTOR COMPANY SERIAL NUMBER AND DATE OF DELIVERY LIST

Serial	Month	Day	Year		Serial	Month	Day	Year		Serial	Month	Day	Year		Serial	Month	Day	Year
500	FEB	13	1942		7130	MAR	20	1942		15080	APR	9	1942		20456	MAY	13	1942
1098	FEB	19	1942		7588	MAR	23	1942		15642	APR	13	1942		20482	APR	17	1942
1100			1942		7663	MAR	23	1942		15933	APR	7	1942		21193	APR		1942
1351	MAR	12	1942		7793			1942		16002	APR		1942		21470	APR	21	1942
1813	MAR	4	1942		8053	MAR	19	1942		16018	APR	9	1942		21756	APR		1942
2038	MAR		1942		8142	MAR	18	1942		16253	MAY	8	1942		21841	APR	30	1942
2154	MAR	2	1942		8171	MAR	19	1942		16522	JAN		1942		21912	APR	28	1942
2172	MAR	3	1942		8228	MAR	28	1942		16944	APR	16	1942		21923	APR	28	1942
2200	FEB	26	1942		8399	MAR	26	1942		17256	APR	16	1942		22219	APR	12	1942
2333	FEB	27	1942		8869	MAR		1942		17257	APR	16	1942		22371	MAY	13	1942
2517	MAR	2	1942		9048	MAR	25	1942		17269	APR	16	1942		22605	APR	29	1942
2518	MAR		1942		9225	MAR	25	1942		17623	APR		1942		22861	MAY	14	1942
2887	MAR		1942		9332	MAR	22	1942		17860	APR	16	1942		22869	MAY	22	1942
2927	MAR	6	1942		9454	MAR	27	1942		18045	APR	22	1942		22891	MAY	15	1942
3308	MAR	4	1942		9666	MAR	26	1942		18179	APR	13	1942		22899	MAY	15	1942
3759	MAR	5	1942		9696	MAR		1942		18266	APR	13	1942		23014	APR	28	1942
4248	MAR	2	1942		9760	MAR	3	1942		18371	MAY	11	1942		23014	APR	28	1942
4395	MAR	6	1942		9804	MAR		1942		18524	APR	23	1942		24340	MAY	1	1942
4407	MAR	16	1942		9919	MAR	27	1942		18562	APR	22	1942		24400	MAY	18	1942
4596	MAR	16	1942		9921	MAR	30	1942		18746	APR	2	1942		24429	MAY	20	1942
5391	MAR	17	1942		10255	MAR	11	1942		19013	APR	17	1942		24694	MAY	15	1942
5415	MAR	16	1942		10405	MAR	10	1942		19018	APR	25	1942		25926	JUN	22	1943
5482	MAR		1942		10877	APR		1942		19025	APR	17	1942		25946	JUN	18	1942
5502	MAR		1942		11079	MAR	27	1942		19067	APR	25	1942		26992	MAY	29	1942
5595	MAR	2	1942		11486	APR	1	1942		19266	APR		1944		27164	MAY	18	1942
5887	MAR	12	1942		11656	APR	2	1942		19688	MAY	14	1942		27276	JUN	2	1942
6331	MAR	16	1942		11678	APR	6	1942		19860	JUL		1942		27433	JUN	1	1942
6436			1942		12494	MAR	31	1942		20085	APR	27	1942		27619	MAY	26	1942
6905	MAR	16	1942		13667	APR	8	1942		20122	APR	29	1942		28760	MAY	13	1942
6976	MAR		1942		13691	APR	4	1942		20198	APR	21	1942		28796	JUN	16	1942
7077	MAR	12	1942		13914	APR	8	1942		20373	APR	17	1942		28861	MAY	14	1942

GPW   GPW   GPW

29091	JUN		1942	41882	JUL		1942	59689	AUG	31	1942	92219	JAN	12	1943
29679	MAY	12	1942	42880	JUL	8	1942	60074	AUG	31	1942	92265	JAN	20	1943
29938	MAY	21	1942	42974	JUL	6	1942	63259	SEP	10	1942	92578	JAN	20	1943
30325	JUN	1	1942	43359	JUL	7	1942	63780	SEP	8	1942	92838	JAN	14	1943
30690	MAY	15	1942	44532	JUL	2	1942	64716	SEP	10	1942	92884	JAN	8	1943
31413	MAY	20	1942	44535	JUL	2	1942	65169	OCT	21	1942	95501	FEB	2	1943
31627	MAY	27	1942	44687	JUL		1942	65685	AUG	12	1942	96250	FEB	4	1943
31672	MAY	27	1942	44843	JUL	3	1942	65948	SEP	15	1942	96821	FEB	10	1943
32030	MAY	27	1942	44989	JUL	1	1942	66669	OCT	21	1942	97250	FEB	10	1943
32037	MAY	27	1942	46162	JUL	7	1942	66891	SEP		1942	98360	FEB	16	1943
32075	MAY	5	1942	46348	JUL	21	1942	70778	OCT	7	1942	99043	FEB	22	1943
34071	JUN	4	1942	47899	JUL		1942	71131	OCT		1942	101969	MAR	3	1943
34185	MAR	29	1942	48305	JUL	16	1942	71854	OCT	13	1942	102063	MAR		1943
34572	AUG	12	1942	48626	JUL	15	1942	72105	OCT	19	1942	102555	MAR	11	1943
34626	MAY	29	1942	48794	JUL	21	1942	73790	OCT	21	1942	103051	FEB	22	1943
35945	JUN	18	1942	48809	JUL	27	1942	73992	OCT		1942	103786	MAR		1943
35946	JUN	18	1942	48979	JUL	24	1942	75640	OCT	29	1942	103810	MAR	30	1943
36541	JUN	4	1942	49440	JUL	30	1942	76157	OCT	28	1942	103827	MAR	30	1943
36986	JUN	22	1942	49623	JUL	23	1942	77985			1942	103951	MAR	22	1943
37139	JUN	23	1942	49623	JUL	23	1942	78228	NOV	19	1942	104250	MAR	29	1943
37197	JUN	10	1942	49860	JUL		1942	80941	NOV	19	1942	104886	APR		1943
37718	JUN	18	1942	50549	JUL	21	1942	81018	NOV		1942	104984	APR	19	1943
37718	JUN	18	1942	50793	JUL	20	1942	82063	NOV	23	1942	105971	MAR	26	1943
38538	JUN	11	1942	51330	JUL	29	1942	83168	NOV		1942	106846	APR	5	1943
38712	JUN	10	1942	51500	JUL	28	1942	84170	DEC	4	1942	107742	MAR	3	1943
38967	JUN	16	1942	52136	JUL	31	1942	84426	DEC	3	1942	108398	APR	7	1943
38979	JUN	12	1942	52203	AUG	3	1942	84563	DEC	9	1942	111026	MAY		1943
39674	JUN	11	1942	52358	AUG	3	1942	84755	DEC		1942	112401	APR	29	1943
40449			1942	55506	AUG	12	1942	86720	DEC	15	1942	112602	MAY		1943
40731	JUN	16	1942	56585	AUG	12	1942	89067	JAN	28	1942	114007	MAY		1943
41196	JUN	25	1942	56586	AUG	12	1942	91321	JAN	6	1943	114036	MAY		1943
41234	JUN	29	1942	56744	AUG	17	1942	91369	JAN	6	1943	114090	APR		1943
41555	JUN	18	1942	57176	AUG	18	1942	92146	JAN	12	1943	114482	APR	30	1943
41837	JUL		1942	57230	AUG	11	1942	92184	JAN	14	1943	114629	MAY	28	1943

GPW   GPW   GPW

Serial	Month	Day	Year		Serial	Month	Day	Year		Serial	Month	Day	Year		Serial	Month	Day	Year
115456	MAY	1	1943		144415	SEP		1943		175302	FEB		1944		206262	JUN		1944
117064	MAY	17	1943		151669	NOV	17	1943		176694	JAN		1944		210718	JUN	13	1944
117138	MAY	18	1943		153898	OCT	21	1943		182647	FEB	25	1944		211691	JUL		1944
117399	MAY	15	1943		158153	NOV	12	1943		186098	MAR		1944		211765	JUL		1944
117657	MAY		1943		158278	NOV	6	1943		194541	MAY	10	1944		212532	JUL		1944
118245	JUN	9	1943		158363	NOV	6	1943		195014	APR	22	1944		213726	JUN	21	1944
118757	JUN	16	1943		158774	NOV	16	1943		195308	JUN		1944		214278	JUL	28	1944
122689	JUN	9	1943		158787	NOV		1943		195515	JUN		1944		214473	JUL	26	1944
124655	JUN	28	1943	**GPW**	159968	NOV	15	1943	**GPW**	196053	APR	13	1944	**GPW**	214743	JUL	31	1944
125095	JUN	29	1943		160020	NOV	23	1943		197429	APR	21	1944		215020	JUL	28	1944
125572	JUL	13	1943		160920	NOV	23	1943		198414	MAY		1944		216003	AUG	14	1944
127040	JUN	14	1943		164626	DEC	7	1943		200584	MAY	12	1944		216144	MAR		1944
127179	JUL		1943		164800	AUG	2	1943		202912	MAY	19	1944		218794	SEP	6	1944
127196	JUL		1943		164800	DEC	8	1943		204203	MAY	31	1944		220584	AUG	24	1944
130591	JUL		1943		165140	DEC	18	1943		204254	JUN	1	1944		222153	JUL		1944
133205	MAY	17	1943		165536	DEC	15	1943		205175	JUN	8	1944		222171	OCT		1944
134259	AUG	12	1943		165625	DEC	12	1943		205592	JUN	7	1944		222185	OCT		1944
142829	SEP		1943		171059	DEC	30	1943		206138	JUN		1944		222197	OCT		1944

The original caption of this US Army Signal Corps photo says it shows Privates Wayne McClung and Francis Phillips of 800 Ord Co, 100th Inf Div installing a new clutch on a very muddy MB at Wolfskirchen, France on 21 February 1945.

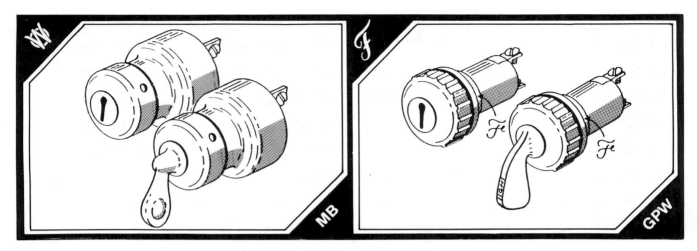

Ignition switches are such an obvious part of any restored military vehicle that it is worthwhile to make sure you have the one appropriate to your ¼ ton. The first MBs and GPWs used switches that took the standard H-700 key. Problems developed when vehicles could not be used because of lost keys, so the intelligent thing was done - the key was eliminated.

MBs up to serial number 202023 (December 1942) used the A-2517 key type ignition switch. After that they used the A-6811 "handle" type ignition switch assembly manufactured by H A Douglas Mfg Co.

Ford GPWs (and the GPA) up to about serial number 89000 (December 1942) used the GPW-3686 key type switch. After that they used the GPW-3686-B "handle" type switch.

The obvious external difference between the Ford and Willys types that one can see with the switches in place are:

A) Ford BEZELS have little bumps around their circumference to make them easy to install and remove while Willys BEZELS have 2 holes in the side so they need to be tightened or loosened with a 1¼ inch spanner wrench.

B) Ford "handles" are flat on the sides and have the letters IGN cast in the front edge. The "handles" on the Willys MB are more rounded in shape. All four styles are depicted above for easy reference. Naturally, Ford switches have a little script F on them (arrow above), cast into the portion that fits inside the dash.

Serial	Mon	Day	Year	Serial	Mon	Day	Year		Serial	Mon	Day	Year		Serial	Mon	Day	Year
222216	OCT		1944	234099	OCT	11	1944		251336	APR		1945		259506	APR		1945
225002	OCT	2	1944	241413	DEC	12	1944		252846	FEB	14	1945		259521	APR		1945
225867	SEP	26	1944	241905	DEC	21	1944		252867	FEB	14	1945		259528	APR		1945
228218	OCT	10	1944	242027	DEC	16	1944		254432	FEB	21	1945		259535			1945
229203	OCT	9	1944	242401	DEC	15	1944		254906	FEB	21	1945		259539	APR		1945
229556	SEP	16	1944	242823	DEC	19	1944		255376	FEB	24	1945		259654	APR		1945
229576	OCT	19	1944	243028	JAN	1	1945		256016	MAR	3	1945		261422	MAR	26	1945
229596	OCT		1944	243405	NOV	29	1944		256365	FEB	26	1945		264267	APR	12	1945
229599	OCT	19	1944	243875	DEC	29	1944		257185	MAR	28	1945		264410	APR		1945
229654	OCT	18	1944	244231	JAN		1945		257215	MAR		1945		264876	APR	5	1945
229880	OCT	19	1944	244508	JAN		1945		257491	MAR	6	1945		265426	APR	16	1945
230310	OCT		1944	246215	JAN		1945		257561	MAR	6	1945		265714	APR	2	1945
230355	OCT	18	1944	246581	JAN		1945		258057	FEB		1945		266206	MAY		1945
230967	OCT	21	1944	249591	JAN	27	1945		258998	MAY	14	1945		266322	APR	23	1945
232051	OCT	10	1944	250985	FEB	3	1945		259116	MAY		1945		266427	APR	24	1945
232933	NOV	2	1944	250986	FEB	3	1945		259145	APR		1945		266487	APR	24	1945

(GPW)

This GPW is the subject of major surgery at the hands of T/5 Arthur Miller and T/4 Daniel O'Brien in the shop of the 880 Ham Ord Co, Namur, Belgium on 3 November 1944. A great example of a "hood star" placed "according to the book".

266547	APR	25	1945
267683	MAY	9	1945
268388	MAY	23	1945
268660	APR		1945
268896	MAY	21	1945
269112	MAY	23	1945
272980	JUL	3	1945
273879	JUN	7	1945
274591	JUL	2	1945
275218	JUL	3	1945
277203	JUL	20	1945
277367	JUL	23	1945

GPW

NOTES ON SERIAL NUMBERS

Many have observed that no universal relationship exists between the serial numbers of jeeps produced and their date of delivery to the government. There are reasons for the mismatches.

1. In Ford's case, they produced jeeps in several factories located thousands of miles apart. An entire run of 100 jeeps from the Richmond, California plant could have been produced (for example) on 3 December 42 with serial numbers of 80950-81050 while another run of 100 could have been produced at the Chester, Pennsylvania plant on 20 November 42 with serial numbers of 84050-84150. In other words, the higher numbers could have been delivered weeks BEFORE the lower numbers were delivered.

2. In both the Willys and Ford plants many units from serial numbered production were removed from the production run for one reason or another (oil leaks, for example) prior to being assigned for delivery. These units were repaired and took their place (and production date) within another later production run of higher serial numbers.

3. As shown elsewhere in this book *rebuild programs* both during and after the war re-assembled jeeps from random piles of components without the slightest consideration for serial numbered parts.

4. Hood numbers are another matter. Once a serial number has been established for a vehicle (from the chassis,

engine or data plate) you can determine the approximate date of and the series of production. Manuals like the Willys TM 10-1186 list the contracts and the quantities of MBs they made *plus* the registration (hood) numbers for those contracts. It is quite easy by simple mathematics to come up with a hood number which *could* be correct for a specific vehicle.

See page 253

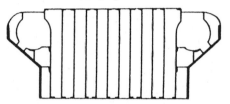

WILLYS SLAT GRILL

All the early jeep prototypes and the first production versions from Bantam (BRC-40), Willys (MA) and Ford (GP) had iron rather than pressed steel radiator guards (grills).

The radiator guards were made of heavy iron wire or light iron bars, arc-welded into a unit at the points where they crossed. They were effective and reasonably easy to produce in limited quantity. On the negative side, they were heavy, they had a

SLAT GRILL ROAD HOG

tendency to break if the welds weren't perfect and they were cumbersome to produce in large quantity.

When Willys won the contract for the first 16,000 real production jeeps on 23 July 1941 they had already greatly modified their original MA into the MB and had adopted a Ford GP type hood and headlights, and simpler fenders. But, unsure of any high volume production to come, they retained an iron grill which required no tooling.

As the first "slat grill" MBs went into production in the early fall of 1941, the reaction to jeeps from Lend-Lease recipients and the US Army convinced the Government that they needed a second source of supply (besides Willys) to produce a standardized version of the jeep. The government selected Ford. Since Willys had been given complete engineering res-

ponsibility for the jeep, they had to provide Ford with the specifications on which Ford would build their GPW. Willys provided their drawings, licenses, patents and other manufacturing information to Ford without cost in the interest of the war effort. It was at this point that Willys adopted the pressed steel grill that was to become the jeep's single most recognizable feature.

As a result of the process by which this change took place, all GPWs were produced with pressed steel grills while the first 25,800 MBs were made with welded iron grills. Of these MB slat grills, only the last 5,112 were made with glove boxes and most of them had a distinctive square outside corner on the bottom of the gas tank sump. The first 3,545 had a shorter windshield assembly than the standard type found on later MBs and on all GPWs. Other factors common to most slat grill MBs that separate them from other MBs are: no blackout marker light on the left front fender, round-base reflectors, a different air cleaner, no spare gas can bracket, no trailer light connector, no chain eyes on the pintle hook, a narrow neck gas tank, a different panel under the driver's seat, unplated cylinder head nuts and so on. All of the differences are pointed out along with the serial number at which the change took place in *TM-10-1186* (1 July 1943) reprinted by the publishers of this book.

SLAVE BATTERY OUTLET RECEPTACLE A-11792

Where was the Slave Battery Outlet Receptacle (A-11792) located on a MB or GPW? Few people have ever seen one, but the Willys-Overland Winterization Field Kit (WKT100) Manual dated March 1944 says it went on the outside of the angular panel on the inside of the right front fender as shown in the illustration.

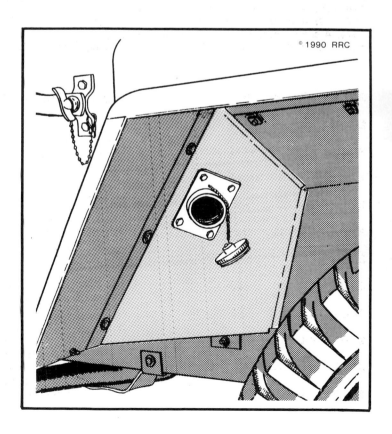

© 1990 RRC

Newly assembled MBs on planks slide to the end of a roller conveyor at Isigny, France just 6 weeks after the D-Day landings on nearby Utah Beach.

GPWs ON MB FRAMES

There is not the slightest doubt that Ford assembled quite a few GPWs on frames built for Willys by A O Smith Company, or at the very least on frames built to Willys specifications.

The Ford/Willys hybrids are among the very rarest of production jeep variants. Usually, they look just like any other early Ford except for the tell-tale tubular Willys front crossmember. They have Ford bodies (often with the Ford name embossed on the rear panel), Ford engines, and even the small parts are all Ford. In most cases the springs and axles are also clearly Ford.

These strange jeeps are often assumed to be motor pool salvage jobs until somebody looks at the top of the left front frame rail between the shock mount and the engine mount bracket. There, between the stars, is a clearly stamped Ford chassis number.

If you think you're looking at a GPW built on a Willys frame and you want to confirm it, take a close look at the plate welded on the *inside* of the left frame horn where the Willys serial number tag *should* have been mounted. The holes for the serial number tag were *predrilled* in this plate *before* the frames were assembled. They should be clean and smooth inside indicating that no drive pins have ever held a Willys serial number tag there.

I'm perfectly comfortable speculating that when Ford switched from the GP to the standardized GPW, they required more frames for production than their internal frame plant could produce. The easy remedy was to order Willys frames from A O Smith Company in Wisconsin.

The well known use of a jeep hood as an altar during religious services is depicted here in an interesting photo taken 21 September 1944. The unit to which the soldiers belong is not known but the cemetery is the WWI American Cemetery at St. Michel, France

FUNNY FORD BLOCKS

Due to a change in casting design at Ford, some of their 1944 engine blocks were sub-standard when produced. These blocks have casting numbers K10-4 to L29-4 (November 10, 1944 to December 29, 1944 and NOT October 10 to November 29 as reported in some sources). Most didn't survive to become collector's items but if you have one be extra careful to use the special shouldered studs Ford made for installing the valve spring cover assembly.

THE JEEPS OF JAMES SESSIONS

James Sessions was during his lifetime (1882-1964) at the forefront among American watercolorists. Educated at the Art Institute of Chicago, his early career gained him great recognition as a western artist.

Over the years his subject matter shifted to seascapes and historical scenes of ships and naval battles. Prior to WWII he was recognized as an authority on camouflage, and with the onset of the war

Sessions was hired by the US Navy as their official battle painter. In this capacity he completed many paintings after viewing then-secret combat movie film.

Among his few commercial clients during the war was Willys-Overland Motors, Inc., of Toledo, Ohio USA. Sessions was commissioned by them to illustrate the claim that, "The sun never sets on the Willys Jeep". He did so with fervor and may have created as many as 60 beautiful paintings

depicting both combat and civilian applications for their famous Jeeps.

Due to the scarceness of the original Sessions paintings we hired acrylic specialist L G Dawes to meticulously copy the master's work from color prints that date back to the 1940s. We then painstakingly color-separated eight of the Dawes paintings to create the prints included in this book.

Page 194

US COAST GUARD GIVES JAPS THE OLD "ONE-TWO"

Painted from an eye-witness account of a US Coast Guardsmen returned from Guadalcanal, this painting depicts the Coast Guard unloading a convoy under Japanese bombing and strafing.

Page 195

JEEP PINCH-HITS FOR A 2½ TON TRUCK

With Nazi planes overhead, a ¼ ton pulls a heavy gun out of the surf and across the beach at Sicily.

Page 198

TERRIFIC!
(ZA-ME-CHA-TEL-NO in Russian)

Zamechatelno is said to have been the standard response of Russian soldiers when asked what they thought of their jeeps. This early painting depicts an advantage the slat-grill MB gave them.

Page 199

HEROIC OFFICERS DARE DEATH FOR MEN

Subtitled "A Salute to the Fighting Men of the US Army Ground Forces", it depicts an incident of the invasion of North Africa in 1942. In an effort to get the French commander at Port Lyautey, Casablanca to surrender, the American commander and an officer-driver attempted to get through to the fortress in a jeep carrying the national flags of France and America and a white flag of truce. Although the attempt failed (the US commander killed and the jeep destroyed) the scene was memorialized by Sessions as an example of "jeep heroism".

Page 202

A JEEP'S-EYE-VIEW OF THE SEABEES IN ACTION

One Seabee shoots down a Japanese Zero while others in jeeps repair the damage to Marsden Matting caused by an earlier bombing raid. In the Solomon Islands of the South Pacific.

Page 203

GIVIN' 'EM HELL AT GUADALCANAL

Marines and soldiers on Guadalcanal Island in the Solomons use a jeep-mounted gun to down Japanese planes.

Page 206

THE JEEP SERVES THE NEEDS OF WAR...AROUND THE GLOBAL CLOCK, by John Howard

Little jeeps positioned at the hour-marks on a clock surrounding the world. In the clouds, tiny post-war jeeps carry out a variety of civilian tasks.

Page 207

SMOKE SCREEN SAVES AMERICAN SOLDIERS IN TUNISIA (Partial)

The original painting told the whole story mentioned in the title. Our picture of an observer in a jeep on a hilltop is only a portion of that original, but was used as we have reproduced it on the cover of a Willys-Overland semi-annual report in 1944.

The painting in the Willys-Overland ad on page 258 is a Sessions and the one in the ad on page 243 is by Horndorf.

REPRINTS

This set of 8 color prints is available from the distributor of this book, printed on high quality art paper in a size of 10" x 12½" (25 cm x 32 cm), suitable for framing. Write for details.

U S Marine Commandant General Holcomb inspecting the deployment of his men on Guadalcanal. Seated behind Holcomb is General Vandegrift and next to him is Colonel Merritt Edson of the Raiders. The jeep has both frame horn hooks and bumper rings common to many USMC jeeps used in the island campaigns. Notice also that the first jeep has no windshield or black-out marker light on the fender. Marine Corps jeeps in combat areas had few or no identifying markings painted on them and were never marked with the white stars common to Army equipment used in the Pacific.

The 4th and 5th Marine Divisions put over 30,000 men ashore on the first day of the battle for Iwo Jima and many of them never got far from the surf. Very heavy Japanese fire and volcanic ash beaches prevented a lot of equipment (including this jeep) from being put to use.

WORTH NOTING

Jeep Horn
When you adjust a jeep horn always have the engine running. The reason is that the battery delivers only 6 volts while the generator delivers 8 volts. This affects the tone of the horn.

Hub Bolts
Left hand wheel hub bolts are identified with an "L" stamped on the threaded end. Left hand nuts have a groove around the hexagonal faces.

Front Springs
Because of the extra weight on the front left side of a MB or GPW the left front spring is heavier and should have a one inch letter "L" painted in white on the bottom side at the front of the second leaf. With a 525 pound (238 kg) load on the left side and a 390 pound (177 kg) load on the right, both front wheels should have a 5/16 inch camber.

Spring Shackels
There are TWO spring shackels on each WWII jeep which have BOTH left and right hand threads. The left part of the shackle is identified by a boss forged onto it. The left threaded portion goes through the *spring eye* on the *left front* and *right rear* spring. The other shackles have right threads top and bottom. The two left hand

threaded shackle bushings in each set are identified by a groove cut around the hexagonal faces.

Squeeky Bushings
Do NOT lubricate squeeking rubber shock absorber bushings on a jeep. The squeek indicates they are moving. Add another flat washer to prevent the movement.

Drain Plugs
The plugs that go in the front floor drains of a jeep should be brass according to TM-10-1513.

Bond Straps
The points where bond straps are bolted to sheet metal (body) parts should be tinned and left unpainted.

"S" Letter
The letter "S" painted on the cowl of jeeps equipped with radio suppression should be centered between the hood and windshield, 1 ¼ inch above the bottom edge of the hood.

Eye Bolts
The safety strap eyebolts on the dash of a WWII era jeep should be oriented horizontally according to the original Willys-Overland engineering drawing updated to 4 June 1945.

THE MESSAGE IN THE LAMPS

UNDER 60 FEET (20 METERS)

The blackout lamps front and rear on WWII era military vehicles such as the jeep were specifically designed to make driving at night in columns easier. They do this by changing their appearance as the distance from viewer to vehicle changes.

The rear blackout lamps are divided into *four* sections side-to-side and from a distance of *less than 60 feet* (20 meters) four distinct points of light are visible to anyone following the vehicle. This is too close for safety.

At distances of 60 to 180 feet (20-50 meters) a rear blackout lamp appears to be two separate points of light to the viewer. This is considered a moderate and safe interval for vehicles driving at night in a column.

At distances between 180 and 800 feet (50-250 meters) on a clear night, a blackout lamp should appear to be a single point of light to an observer and simply indicates a vehicle ahead.

The blackout lamps at the front of WWII era vehicles are divided into *two* sections which are visible as two points of light at distances of 60 feet (20 meters) or less. At greater distances they appear to be a single source of light.

One of the US Army suggestions for better night vision in a column was to open the windshield. Military columns moving at night necessarily travel at very, very slow speeds.

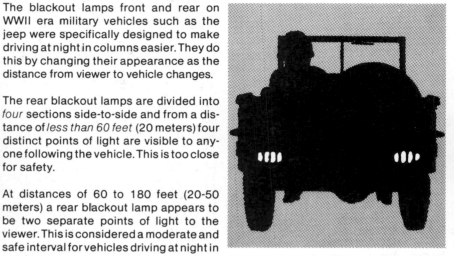

UNDER 60 FEET (20 METERS)

OVER 60 FEET (20 METERS)

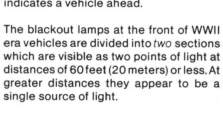

OVER 60 FEET (20 METERS)

OVER 60 FEET (20 METERS)

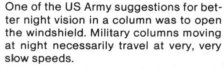

A-6142

OVER 180 FEET (60 METERS)

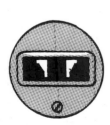

A-1436 (L)

The blackout driving lamp on the other hand, was intended to create a beam of light that would allow the vehicle operator to see where he was going with minimum risk that the beam would be observed by the enemy above or in the area of the vehicle. While it is a great theory, the beam emitted by the lamp was no substitute for real lights or daylight.

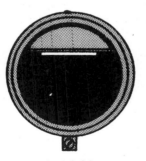

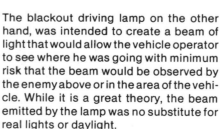

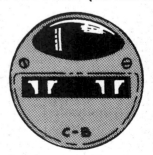

A-1064 (L)

197

The office of the Army-Navy Liquidation Commissioner was established in February 1945 to oversee the sale, donation, or other disposal of all US property declared surplus. In the period from 1 June 1944 to 1 February 1946 the War Department put $9.79 billion worth of material of all kinds in the surplus category for disposal by the Commissioner. The jeeps shown here were declared surplus in November 1945 at Cheltenham, England where they were sold.

EUROPEAN SURPLUS AND

The American Occupation Forces in Germany were almost as hard on jeeps as the war was. A huge jeep rebuilding facility was established at Esslingen, Germany where this photo shows the collection area for dead jeeps outside the rebuild shops. All vehicles were completely disassembled so that production line techniques could be applied to the rebuild process.

Top photo shows German civilian workers at Esslingen sorting front and rear end assemblies in preparation for rebuilding. The bottom photo shows rows of thoroughly reconditioned jeeps ready for assignment to units. All jeeps were run over an 8 mile test course prior to certification. Notice the pile of MB/GPW bodies stacked across the street from the jeeps. Is it any wonder so few jeeps have matching chassis, body, and engine numbers?

REBUILDING PROGRAMS

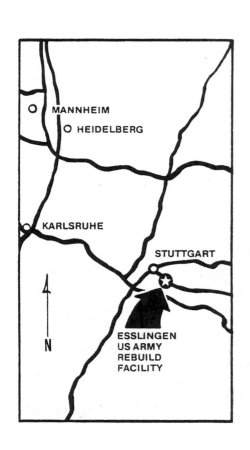

MANNHEIM
HEIDELBERG
KARLSRUHE
STUTTGART
ESSLINGEN US ARMY REBUILD FACILITY
N

CAMOUFLAGE ON US JEEPS IN WWII

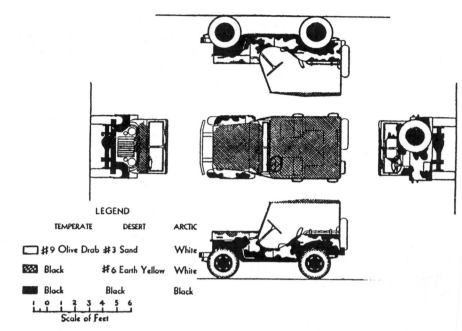

LEGEND

	TEMPERATE	DESERT	ARCTIC
☐	#9 Olive Drab	#3 Sand	White
▓	Black	#6 Earth Yellow	White
■	Black	Black	Black

Scale of Feet

FIGURE 10.—Camouflage pattern for bantam car.

Though rarely seen on restorations, camouflage paint jobs were certainly allowed for according to *FM 5-21 (Engineer Field Manual, Camouflage Painting of Vehicles and Field Equipment)* dated 7 October 1942 from which this drawing was taken.

The manual guidelines include this advice:
1) Patterns should be irregular.
2) Patterns should extend over the edges and around the corners in order to obscure outline and form.
3) Objects should generally be painted darker on top and lighter below.
4) Size of pattern should be determined by distance from hostile observation.
5) Vehicle color (OD) makes a good base color and should be used with black and a carefully selected third color.
6) The paint could be applied with a brush or spray equipment.

It is known from a photo in the July 1941 issue of *National Geographic* (p 25) and in *Life* magazine of 1 September 1941 (p 57) that at least one jeep and 37 mm gun were camouflage painted during the 1941 Summer War Games. It is likely that many more were as well. It is certain from period photos that the US Marine Corps used camouflage painted jeeps in the Pacific during WWII.

Camouflage painting of US vehicles was fairly common in the Italian campaign and during the Winter of 1944-1945 in the area of the Battle of the Bulge in Belgium and Luxembourg. NOTE the nomenclature under the illustration - "bantam car".

Camouflaged GP above was photographed during the 1941 Summer War Games while the camouflaged ¼ ton at left was photographed during USMC amphibious exercises in New Zealand in 1942.

204

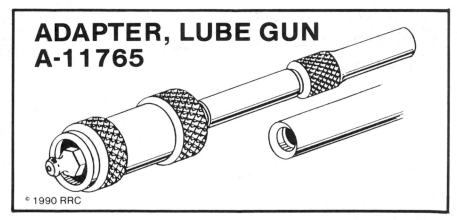

ADAPTER, LUBE GUN
A-11765

© 1990 RRC

This 5½ inch (140 mm) long tool is an adapter to make it possible to lubricate the universal joints on the propeller shafts on a MB or GPW. It extends the reach of the hand grease gun.

A jeep provides mobility and firepower to a unit of the US 103rd Infantry Division which had taken fire from students at a German officer school near Scharnitz, Austria on 1 May 1945.

Medics tend a GI wounded in Coutances, France on 31 July 1944 after his jeep struck a German mine. The wreckage in the left foreground is the rear cross member, bumperettes and rear rack from the victim's GPW. The two convoy maintenance jeeps parked at the right have extra Blackout Driving Lamps on their right front fenders.

FILTERETTES

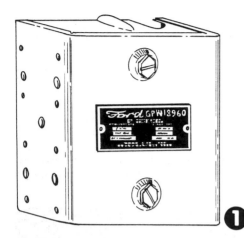

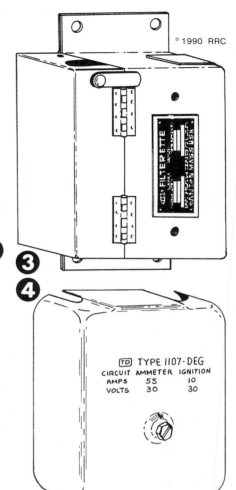

With all the emphasis the US Government placed on reducing the weight of the ¼ ton, the filterettes found on MBs and GPWs wouldn't have been there unless they were necessary. These heavy little boxes contain a coaxial capacitor to filter out "hash" that would otherwise jam the radio circuit. It is clear that radios were intended for jeeps right from the start as the very first of them off the assembly line were fully equipped with radio suppression equipment.

The largest component in this group is the filterette which is usually found bolted to the passenger side of the toe board under the dash. There is evidence to suggest that the unit was also mounted on the inside of the right front fender (under the fuel filter) on at least several thousand of the Willys slat grill MBs.

The radio suppression system underwent a change at MB serial number 288,835 when the large filter was dropped and smaller filters were attached to the coil stud, ignition switch, starter motor, voltage regulator and the generator. At the same time (late winter 1943) ground straps 2, 5,

6, 8, 9, 10, 12, 13, 14, 15, 16, 21 and 22 were eliminated as unnecessary, and a number of internal tooth washers were placed in the system to insure good grounding.

Filterettes were made by Erie Resistor Corporation, Erie, PA, Tobe-Deutschmann Corporation, Canton, MA, Solar Manufacturing Company, Bayonne, NJ, Sprague Specialties Company, North Adams, MA, and perhaps others. Naturally, some are marked Ford but were built for Ford by the principal contractors.

The filterettes shown are typical examples of principal types. They are:

1. Ford GPW 18960 as made by Sprague with their part number JX-17, MLL 134739.
2. Tobe-Deutschmann 1107DE.
3. A Tobe-Deutschmann with a hinged access door as found in the engine compartment on a slat grill MB.
4. Tobe-Deutschmann 1107 DEG.

The Willys-Overland part number for the filterette is A-5980 and for Ford it is GPW 18960.

WRENCH, FLUTED SOCKET HEAD (FOR TRANSMISSION) A-1492

This odd looking little wrench is necessary for removing, installing or adjusting the shifting forks on the shift rails in the Warner T-84 transmissions in MBs and GPWs.

LIGHT SWITCH TAG

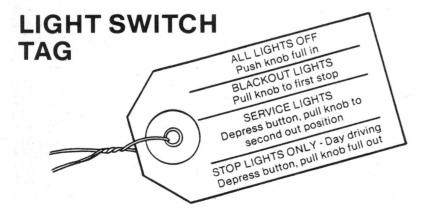

ALL LIGHTS OFF
Push knob full in
BLACKOUT LIGHTS
Pull knob to first stop
SERVICE LIGHTS
Depress button, pull knob to second out position
STOP LIGHTS ONLY - Day driving
Depress button, pull knob full out

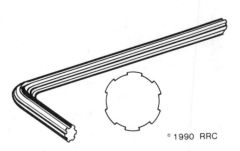

© 1990 RRC

208

FRANZ UCKO AND HIS JEEPS

Franz Ucko, now of St. Paul, Minnesota, was born in Beuthen, Germany. When he fled to Manila in 1939 he was a Mechanical Engineer with a strong interest in photography. During the Japanese occupation of the Philippines, he served as a photographer with a local guerilla group. When American forces returned, he volunteered as a civilian photographer with the 37th Infantry Division. Later that year he was inducted and when he came up for a direct commission, it was learned that he wasn't an American. Arrangements were made for him to be sworn as an American citizen along with a group of Filipino Scouts and he got his commission. He stayed on in the Philippines for a while after the war was over. He retired from Control Data Corporation in 1985.

Franz Ucko is shown here with one foot solidly planted on the step of his Ford GPW jeep while taking photos in a previously unexplored and unmapped area of Luzon, Philippine Islands in 1945. The Nigritos (Philippine pygmys) with him seem oblivious to the high technology they're sitting on.

TWO GENERALS AND THEIR JEEPS

Japanese Lt Gen Yamashita seen saluting as he leaves his jeep to attend surrender ceremonies in Baguio, Philippine Islands in 1945.
General Douglas McArthur and Maj Gen William H Geightler (CO 37th Inf Div) have a discussion while McArthur sits in a jeep. The photo was taken near the invasion site on the Lingayen Gulf, Luzon. Franz Ucko (L) looks on.

US Army Photographer Franz Ucko filming an episode of The March of Time in the Philippines after the war ended. With him is Dr Cochanco, Dean of the Philippine Agricultural School. The GPW has had the windshield modified to provide more headroom.

CAPSTAN WINCH

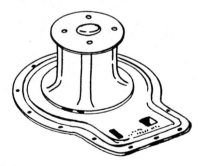

While it is not a common accessory on military jeeps of the WWII period, the capstan winch is a highly desirable one because of its utility and because it contributes additional interest right up at the front of any vehicle that has one. The nautical style of the vertical cylinder (or spool) of the capstan winch is itself unusual in an era when many people have only seen a reel type winch.

The winch used on the MB/GPW is the same as had been standard on the GPA and Weasel (Braden J2/A-9232) and no doubt somewhere along the line somebody decided it would improve the utility of the ¼ ton. By March 1944 the Government had a field kit available which could be fitted to either a MB or a GPW. There are slight differences in how the winch bracket is mounted on a Willys or a Ford but in both cases the front of the jeep is disassembled to install the winch kit. New front springs and a new bell crank came in the kit.

The capstan is a vertically mounted spool which is driven by a worm and worm gear that takes its power from a shaft connected directly to the crankshaft pulley on the front of the engine. In use, the winch is intended to free the vehicle it is mounted on if the wheels alone do not have sufficient traction to move it. It is a two-man operation in most circumstances.

One attaches a ¾ inch or 1 inch rope to any immovable object nearby the stuck jeep (a tree for example) then loops the rope twice around the spool on the winch. While one man operates the stuck vehicle, another stands off to the side and keeps tension on the loose end of the rope as the winch pulls the vehicle forward. It is a somewhat slow and artful process (19 ft. per minute) but it works. When finished, the capstan drive is disengaged by moving a shifting lever. Naturally, the jeep can be used as the "immovable object" and the winch can be used to pull another vehicle, to move heavy equipment, etc.

WWII ended before many of the capstan winch field kits could reach the field. As a result the kits were a very common surplus item in the 1950s in the price range of $15.00 - $20.00

See also page 237.

HULL M4 COMPASS ON A JEEP

© 1990 RRC

HR

Hull Manufacturing of Warren, OH was a major producer of M4 compasses for the US Army during and after WWII. The advertisement above is typical of those Hull placed in magazines (this one from *Popular Science*, Nov 42) to keep their image in front of American consumers.

The illustration shows the compass in the OD painted military form. The compass body was bakelite and had a bulbous lens on the front. An adjusting screw on the side and another on the front made it easy to properly orient the ring-type direction indicator inside the body. The military version was the standard brown bakelite unit painted OD but with a military mounting bracket that gave the compass better shock resistance than the civilian unit.

The mounting bracket on the military version of the Hull compass was simply a rod set in a piece of black rubber hose held by a small bent-metal bracket as shown here. The rod was attached to the back of the compass with a set screw.

The photo below depicts one of these M4 Hull compasses in use on a US Military Police jeep in France in 1944. The Restricted Signal Corps copy on the back of the original photo says:

"SC 196495
A two-way radio helps MPs to patrol a city in France with greater ease. Here, two members of the prowl car, Cpl. Floyd R. Mace (left), Smith Center, KS, and Pfc. Robert J. Eaves, Birmingham, AL, listen to a call coming from headquarters. 11/ 14/44"

Who would have guessed at the time, that a half-century later the unique thing about the photo would be the Hull M4 compass hanging from the windshield of the jeep?

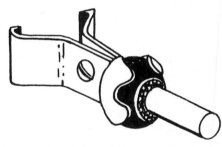

A second variation of the mounting bracket shown above is a shaft mounted in rubber inside a brass ball. The ball is clamped in a bracket that attaches to the center divider of the windshield on a MB or GPW. New military compasses have also been found in standard brown and black bakelite.

Based on comments from knowledgable readers of volume 1 of this book, here is the correct sequence of the use of the different types of footman loops found on MBs and GPWs. Types B and C are identical.

WILLYS/FORD TEARDOWN REPORT
APRIL 1943

The concept of Ford/Willys interchangeability is not a new one or one strictly of concern to the restorers who preserve old jeeps. As the prime contractor for ¼ ton trucks for the US Government during WWII, Willys-Overland was very concerned about how parts from Ford vehicles would interchange with those they put into MBs, and determined to make Ford comply with Willys engineering. The report that follows was compiled by C W Jones and D D Stone of the Willys-Overland Research Department in Toledo, Ohio on 19 April 1943.

They took apart a Ford GPW built in November of 1942 and then assembled the pieces into a MB of unknown, but presumably similar vintage. The report is extremely valuable to all jeep restorers. As an example, item 11 states that only GPWs should have a *one piece* skid plate and exhaust pipe guard. At least 90% of the MB restorations I've looked at have a *FORD* skid plate and exhaust pipe guard. The word "Jeep" in this early report was capitalized as in the tradename.

WILLYS OVERLAND MOTORS INC.
RESEARCH DEPARTMENT

Subject: Comparison between Ford and Willys Overland built Jeeps for interchangeability.

A Ford Jeep, Serial No. GWP-79160, was loaned to this Department by the Ordnance Department, United States Army, for detailed comparison as to inter-changeability of all parts with the Willys production MB Jeep. To make this comparison

the two Jeeps were dismantled item by item and each assembly and sub-assembly was tried on the other manufacturers vehicle for fit and inter-changeability.

This included first, all of the major assemblies, such as body, sheet metal engine, transmission, transfer cases, axles, gasoline tank etc.

The corresponding sub-assemblies were then placed beside each other and dismantled item by item and the component parts checked for inter-changeability.

No important discrepancies were found in the several weeks time required for the complete check, but there were a few differences that should be noted, and these are as follows.

1. The Ford body dash brace is not like the Willys (see photographs). This does not interfere with the inter-changeability of bodies, but it was found to cause some trouble in the early development of a suitable mounting for a stove required for cold starting. A change of location for the stove eliminated the discrepancy.

2. The Ford frame is somewhat different in construction than the Willys frame and requires special treatment in mounting the starting stove referred to in (1) above.

3. The Ford hood does not have a stringer across the front on the underside, and is not as rigid in construction as the Willys.

4. The transfer case sliding gear out of the Willys transfer case output would not fit on the spline of the Ford transfer case

output shaft. This was found to be due to the Willys shaft being oversize on the outer dia.. This has since been corrected by Warner Gear Company. Sliding gears are a selected fit on this shaft so no service difficulties should be experienced.

The following differences are points where the Ford Jeep deviated from the blueprint specifications and the Willys-Overland construction. These points were brought to the attention of the Engineering representative of Ford Motor Company on 26 February 1943.

1. The Ford gun mount checked 7" x 10". This is smaller than called for on blueprint No. 1151. Also, holes were not like the print.

2. Front spring rear brackets on the frame were approximately 3/32" closer to the center cross member than called for on blueprint No. 1142. This located the engine too close to the front frame cross member.

3. Radiator bracket holes on the front frame cross member were ½" in diameter, drawing No. 1142 calls for ⅝" diameter.

4. Frame center cross member holes were elongated. Drawing No. 406 specifies two holes 13/32" in diameter.

5. Ford left and right fenders had two bolts at the step bracket, Willys had one. This doesn't affect inter-changeability.

6. Ford radiator uses loose carriage bolts to mount it to the frame. Willys

FOOTMAN LOOPS

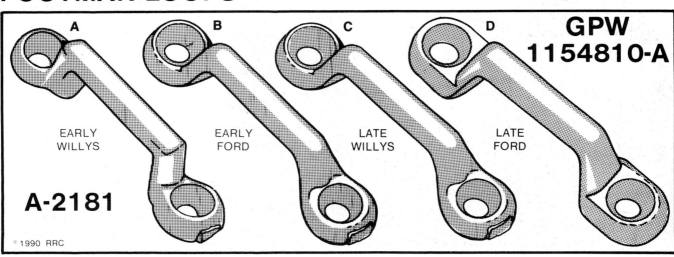

A
EARLY
WILLYS

B
EARLY
FORD

C
LATE
WILLYS

D
LATE
FORD

GPW
1154810-A

A-2181

© 1990 RRC

radiator has studs assembled in bottom of bracket.

7. Ford had no wood spacer on the driver's seat between floor and gas tank shield. This is specified and used on the Willys.

8. The Ford wiring harness on the left side passes through a hole in the body brace so that it might be squeezed against the toe-board by a brake pedal.

9. The Ford battery tray is removable from the frame and is different in design. The Ford battery tray flange should be flared out more to give clearance at the bulged corner of the Auto-lite battery to avoid the chance of battery case damage.

10. The Ford exhaust pipe is different in construction than the Willys, it being attached to the exhaust manifold by a plate welded to the pipe. The Willys exhaust pipe is reinforced where it is supported by a flanged collar.

11. The Ford skid plate and exhaust pipe guard are made from one stamping.

12. On the sample Ford as submitted, no rear body reinforcements at the side of the tool compartment had been added.

13. The rear seat did not contain the tire pump bracket.

14. The Ford connecting rod is different in design from the Willys, the bolts being forged integral in the rod. However as a complete assembly they are interchangeable.

15. The Ford battery ground strap was 3" longer than the Willys. This does not affect inter-changeability.

16. The Ford body bolts are 1/8" longer than Willys.

17. The body bolt tapping block under the gas tank is for 16 threads per inch instead of 24 as called for.

18. Ford starter switch is ½" shorter than Willys. This does not affect inter-changeability.

19. There were some slight advantages in the wiring harness of relative unimportance as the wiring harnesses were interchangeable. However, no snap connector terminals on the Ford were soldered. All Willys connectors were crimped and soldered.

20. The Ford had only one brake line clamp on the front axle. The Willys used two clamps at this point.

21. The Ford oil gauge rod was improperly marked, it being ⅝" too low.

22. The rear motor insulator did not have the reinforcements as shown by changed drawing.

23. The Ford clutch driven disc facings were not tightly riveted to the disc. A new driven disc was installed.

24. The Ford generator to bracket attaching bolts (going through rubber) had only one large washer on each bolt. There are two required.

25. The Ford manifold was not drilled for the ventilator valve. (Change had not yet been accomplished).

26. The Ford air cleaner shield attaching to the frame on the right side is fastened by two 5/16-24 bolts. The Willys uses ¼-

28 for attaching the shield to the frame rail.

27. The Ford shock absorber washers for retaining the rubber bushings on the shaft were only 1/16" thick. Washers ⅛" thick are specified.

28. The Ford front cross member bond straps are 4" long. Willys bond straps are 3" long, and are not interchangeable with Ford because of different location of attaching bolts.

A few points in which the Ford is different than the Willys which might be considered an advantage from an assembly standpoint were as follows:

1. The front muffler bolt is 5/16-24 x ⅞, screwed into a tapping block in the body instead of a carriage bolt through the floor.

2. The horn and gas gauge circuit breaker brackets are together and bolted to the body brace with one bolt. These are spot-welded on the Willys body brace and are less accessible.

3. The gas gauge rubber cap on the gasoline tank is assembled with the wire through the end of the boot. This prevents the cap working up.

4. The Ford air cleaner brackets have tapping blocks in the dash for the two lower bolts.

5. The engine crankcase drain plug base is assembled on the inside of the oil pan.

6. The Ford clutch release tube frame bracket has two tapping blocks for attachment.

The pad on the inside of the left frame rail where the master brake cylinder mounts is radically different on Ford and Willys frames as shown here.

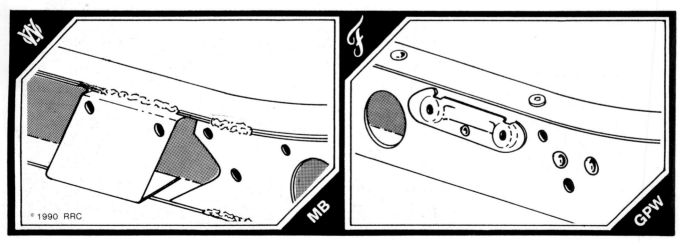

7. The Ford master brake cylinder bolts have tapping blocks in the frame for attachment.

Inspection of the Ford assembly showed the following:

1. The engine oil pan contained some metal cuttings and a slight amount of dirt.

2. The Ford engine oil pump showed indications of dirt having gone through the gears, they being slightly scratched and pitted.

3. The transmission case contained some metal cuttings, some of which had become imbedded in the countershaft bushing and the thrust washer. The countershaft and sliding gears were also chipped at the ends of the teeth.

The axle assemblies were sent to the Spicer Manufacturing Company for disassembling and inspection and the electric equipment was all sent to the Electric Auto-Lite Company for inspection and test. These assemblies were reported as being similar to and interchangeable with similar parts made for the Jeep.

The following special service kits were tried on the Ford Jeep for fit and were found to assemble on the Ford Jeep in the same manner as on the Willys Jeep, except as noted.

(1) Project No. 1187, Part No. A-6940, Desert Cooling Kit.

(2) Project No. 232, Part No. A-11249, Desert Cooling Surge Tank Shield Kit.

(3) Project No. 1217, Part No. A-7189, Cold Starting Stove Kit (Slightly different procedure is required for assembly on the Ford Jeep and this is covered in the installation instructions).

(4) Project No. 1167, Part No. A-6544, Trailer Equipment Conversion Kit.

(5) Project No. 243, Part No. AE-11322, Trailer Electric Plug Cover Kit.

(6) Project No. 1274, Part Nos. A-7868, A-8105, Tow Bar (Installation).

(7) Project No. 1312, Part No. A-8293, Generator, 55 Ampere, P.T.O. Field Kit.

(continued next page)

Payday in Rome on the hood of a jeep. This 3rd Infantry Division version of the famous ¼ ton is highly modified. In addition to armor and armament (note the .50 cal MG extending over the chopped windshield) it has a reversed German BO lamp mounted on the right front fender. The US Army had the world's largest payroll during WWII, disbursing over a billion dollars per week.

(EDITOR'S NOTE: In reading this report and the chart below one can't help but notice that in item 21 on the previous page, the Ford dipstick indicated more oil than was actually in the crankcase. The chart below says that Ford engine assemblies were found to be 7 pounds lighter than Willys engine assemblies. Could this be part of the reason good Ford engine blocks are so hard to find these days?)

(Report continued)

Comparitive weights of the two cars including tools, tire pump, two sets of chains, top, side curtains, windshield boot, light covers, and spare tire and wheel: Ford 2340 lbs.   Willys 2337 lbs.

Direct comparison of a number of items of the two cars showed comparitive weights as follows:

	FORD	WILLYS
1. Hood assembly	32.00 lbs.	32.00 lbs.
2. L.F. Fender assy. (with B.O. driving lamp)	20.00 lbs.	20.00 lbs.
3. R.F. Fender	16.00 lbs.	17.00 lbs.
4. Rad. brush guard & head lamp assy.	22.00 lbs.	22.00 lbs.
5. Radiator and cap	23.00 lbs.	23.50 lbs.
6. Radiator brace rod	.56 lbs.	.56 lbs.
7. Radiator hose, connector tube, clamps	1.87 lbs.	2.11 lbs.
8. Battery (Ford Exide EH15H) (Willys Willard 15H)	53.50 lbs.	49.00 lbs.
9. Air cleaner (inc. oil, both Oakes)	7.62 lbs.	7.81 lbs.
10. Windshield assy. (complete)	42.00 lbs.	42.00 lbs.
11. Right front seat assy.	20.00 lbs.	23.00 lbs.
12. Left front seat assy.	22.00 lbs.	24.00 lbs.
13. Rear seat assy.	23.00 lbs.	26.00 lbs.
14. Steering gear (pittman arm, tube & shaft assy.) (less wheel)	15.00 lbs.	16.00 lbs.
15. Steering wheel	3.70 lbs.	3.50 lbs.
16. Horn assy.	2.18 lbs.	2.19 lbs.
17. Pedal pad assy. Clutch & Brake	2.00 lbs.	2.00 lbs.
18. Gas tank assy. (cap extension & gauge assy.)	22.00 lbs.	24.00 lbs.
19. Muffler assy. (Att. parts and insulator)	7.75 lbs.	7.37 lbs.
20. Skid plate (Ford 1 stamping) (Willys 2 stampings)	10.75 lbs.	10.00 lbs.
21. Exhaust pipe assy.	4.50 lbs.	4.00 lbs.
22. Rear prop. shaft assy.	8.25 lbs.	9.25 lbs.
23. Front prop. shaft assy.	7.40 lbs.	7.25 lbs.
24. Body less seats, gas tank, air cleaner	310.00 lbs.	306.00 lbs.
25. Engine assy, trans., transfer case, carb., complete with starter, generator, coil and all electrical fittings and wire, filter. (no oil in engine)	547.00 lbs.	557.00 lbs.
26. Engine complete, less trans., and transfer case	425.00 lbs.	432.00 lbs.
27. Transmission (att. parts)	43.00 lbs.	45.00 lbs.
28. Transfer case (att. parts)	79.00 lbs.	80.00 lbs.
29. Bell housing	19.00 lbs.	19.50 lbs.
30. Generator (Ford makes own)	31.00 lbs.	32.00 lbs.
31. Starter	17.50 lbs.	17.00 lbs.
32. Cylinder head	24.00 lbs.	23.50 lbs.
33. Cylinder block & stud assy. (inc. bearing caps)	134.00 lbs.	140.25 lbs.
34. Flywheel	24.50 lbs.	24.52 lbs.
35. Crankshaft	42.00 lbs.	41.06 lbs.
36. Camshaft	7.12 lbs.	7.09 lbs.
37. Two front springs	40.00 lbs.	39.50 lbs.
38. Two rear springs	53.00 lbs.	53.00 lbs.
39. Torque reaction spring assy.	10.00 lbs.	9.00 lbs.
40. Front axle assy. (with grease)	212.00 lbs.	212.00 lbs.
41. Rear axle assy. (with grease)	149.00 lbs.	151.00 lbs.
42. Spare tire bracket nuts, lock	3.56 lbs.	3.56 lbs.
43. One tire and wheel assy. (6.00 x 16 Goodyear, 6 ply, Willys) (6.00 x 16 Ford, 6 ply, Ford)	58.00 lbs.	58.00 lbs.

END OF REPORT

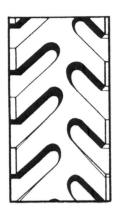 

TIRES & TUBES

MILITARY in 9/16 inch (14 mm) letters, WWII

One of the interesting features of the distinctive 100 lug non-directional tread (NDT) tires that came on jeeps, is the many firms that made them both during and after WWII. Everyone in the tire business was busy making 6.00 x 16 NDT tires.

The standard versions of NDT tires made during WWII contained quite a bit of information written on the sidewalls. In addition to the makers name and/or logo was the size; 6.00 - 16 6 ply Heavy Duty; Inflate to 30 lbs.; MILITARY; and data regarding the production lot number. Original tubes had much of the same information on them plus the notation WAR TUBE.

While they are probably unsafe to drive any distance, an original WWII NDT tire as a spare is a wonderful addition to any restoration.

INFLATE TO 30 LBS., WWII

GOODYEAR ALL SERVICE, WWII

6.00-16 6 PLY HEAVY DUTY, WWII

GOODYEAR WAR TUBE, WWII

FIRESTONE GROUND GRIP

I tried, but I just couldn't leave this photo out of the book. It's not a combat photo, but a movie "still" from the 1949 Metro-Goldwyn-Mayer picture "Battleground". In spite of the fake snow a close inspection of the original photo reveals all the gauges are missing. Could this be an early Van Wicklin prop?

KELLY Springfield, dated 1951

ALLSTATE (SEARS) **N.D.T.,** postwar

KANT KS SLIP

COOPER TIRE & RUBBER CO.

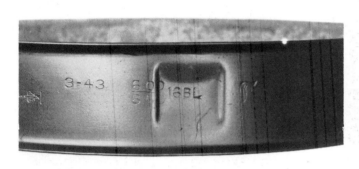

Firestone Bead Lock Ring dated **3-43**

GOODYEAR AIRWHEEL

This photo depicts a key difference between the WWII style NDT tires and the style produced later: The NOS Goodyear at the left has sharply pointed slots between the lugs while the postwar tire on the right has blunt slots.

FORD SCRIPT TIRES

According to Ford historian Lorin D Sorensen the last Ford script tire made was a 6.00 x 16 NDT that came off the tire line in Dearborn on 1 December 1942. The entire Ford tire and tube plant had been purchased by the US Government which packed it up and shipped it to the Soviet Union. As far as is known it was never reassembled and put to use after arrival.

Based on this date, it is very unlikely that any GPW delivered after January 1943 had Ford script tires. Ford purchased tires from Firestone after closing their own plant.

Many people have asked to see a photo of the pliers that came in the tool kit with a WWII jeep. Here is one from a Ford GPW tool kit and shown just above it is a GPW crank illustrating that both have the Ford script name and the logo MH of the company that made them.

Notice that the top handle of the pliers has a screwdriver bit on the end (GK).

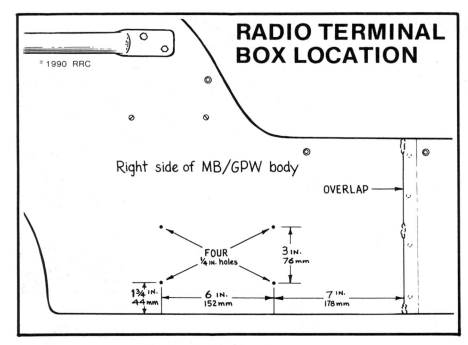

RADIO TERMINAL BOX LOCATION

© 1990 RRC

Right side of MB/GPW body

OVERLAP →

FOUR ¼ IN. holes

3 IN. 76 mm

1¾ IN. 44 mm

6 IN. 152 mm

7 IN. 178 mm

After MB serial number 217543 a lot of jeeps came equipped with a Radio Terminal Box Assembly connected to the electrical system. If you want one on your MB or GPW this drawing will show you exactly where to put the holes.

FRONT-END SHIMMY? One of the main causes is the lack of lubrication of the bell crank. The result is a bell crank shaft with a reverse impression of the bell crank needle bearings all around it as shown on the left in this photo. Well lubricated replacement bearings and shaft do wonders for this problem. The other worn-out shaft in the picture is a transfer case intermediate gear shaft which created plenty of vibration.

The drawings on the next page are not intended to be a complete depiction of all the weapon scabbards used with jeeps. Rather, they are typical of some which were used. GIs were very inventive in rigging this equipment and attaching it to vehicles, so modified scabbards are common.

Number 4 is an arsenal modification of a WWI scabbard for a 30.06. A brass throat was added to the side of this leather scabbard to protect the operating rod handle of the M-1 rifle. The markings below each drawing are the marks of the contractors who made them for the Government as found on samples.

Number 6 of course, is the universal rifle carrier which was attached to the windshield panel on many jeeps during WWII.

It was announced in the original Army Motors in October of 1942.

The paragraph below is copied from the United States Army Driver's Manual (TM 10-460) dated May 6, 1942. Still good advice half a century later!

fit. If the delay ....
ble, with the officer under whose direction you ....
or one of his assistants.

2. **YOUR VEHICLE** is a carefully engineered piece of machinery, easy to operate but easier to damage or destroy by carelessness and neglect. Even the "jeep" (¼-ton truck) is a high-powered machine. Treat it with respect.

3. **YOU AND YOUR VEHICLE.**—As a soldier you pay particular attention to your equipment, clothes, and rifle or pistol. .... in keeping them clean, neat, orderly, ... for per-

WEAPON SCABBARDS

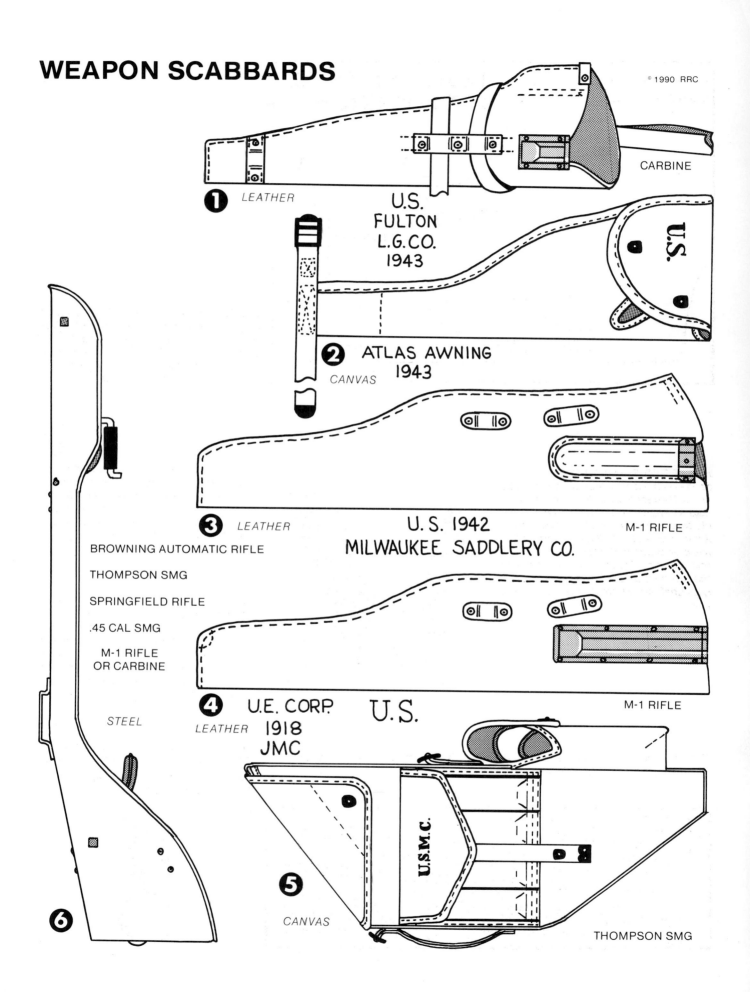

© 1990 RRC

❶ *LEATHER* CARBINE

U.S. FULTON L.G.CO. 1943

U.S.

❷ *CANVAS* ATLAS AWNING 1943

❸ *LEATHER* U.S. 1942 M-1 RIFLE

MILWAUKEE SADDLERY CO.

BROWNING AUTOMATIC RIFLE

THOMPSON SMG

SPRINGFIELD RIFLE

.45 CAL SMG

M-1 RIFLE OR CARBINE

STEEL

❹ *LEATHER* U.E. CORP. 1918 JMC U.S. M-1 RIFLE

❺ *CANVAS* U.S.M.C. THOMPSON SMG

❻

FORD
SAFETY GLASS

© 1990 RRC

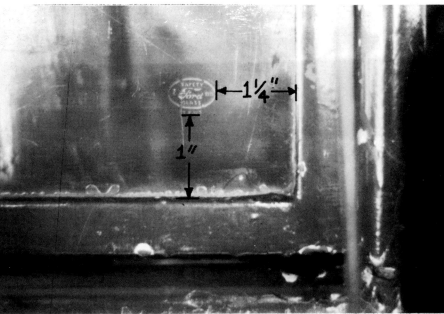

¾ inch Ford logo on GPW glass.

INSIDE view above

OUTSIDE view left

The logo Ford was using to mark the glass they made was the oval shown above with the word Ford written through the center. A mask in this shape was made by punching the image through old Ford promotional movie film (Henry was very thrifty). The mask was held tightly to the glass and the logo was sandblasted through the openings in the mask.

Because the logo also contained a manufacturing code, it changed monthly. Here is how the code worked:

At the left side of the word Ford was a MONTH - letter A for January through L for December. At the right of the word Ford were two YEAR letters, D for the 4 in 194- and A,B,C,D or E for the final number 1,2,3,4 or 5. Thus a code *C Ford DC* would be used on glass made in March 1943. The letters below the oval logo on GPW glass should be AS-F-WS which stands for *American Standard-Ford-Windshield*. Windshield in Ford parlance meant safety plate glass.

Ford GPWs, of course, came with Ford glass in the windshields. The conspicuous marking of the glass with a Ford logo was simply a continuation of Ford's obsession with marking parts with their name or initial.

Henry Ford had built his first glass plant in Highland Park, Michigan in 1921 after experiencing supply problems from his glass vendors. The number of closed-body Model Ts he was able to produce was actually limited by the amount of glass he could get, and Ford was very intolerant of such problems. By the mid-1920s he had become one of the world's largest producers of glass.

With the Model A Ford in 1928 Ford became the first low-price car manufacturer in America to put safety glass in the

windshields of all the cars he made. The popularity of the Model A required Ford to once again buy glass from companies like Libbey-Owens-Ford (no relation) and Pittsburgh Plate Glass, but not for long. By 1936 Ford owned the state-of-the-art laminated plate safety glass factory in America, and was using his own product in the front and rear windows of all the cars and trucks he made. The side windows used Ford safety sheet glass.

(It should be noted that plate glass is actually ground smooth after it is rolled out and is relatively distortion free. Sheet glass on the other hand is not ground, but used just as it is rolled out, and thus can distort an image seen through it. Safety glass of either type was made by laminating a thin sheet of vinyl acetate between two sheets of glass).

From a restoration perspective, GPW glass should probably have a date code that shows the glass was produced *prior* to the date the jeep was delivered. Fortunately for ¼ ton freaks there are people who sell kits with which a restorer can etch very good replicas of the correct Ford logos on new glass. These people advertise in Ford V-8 Club publications. The original logos I've examined have been located on the inside of the glass in the lower right hand corner as shown in the upper photograph above.

The rear jeep in the photo at the right has a plate affixed to the body just above the rear wheel opening. Usually the plates in this position contained information about a group (such as a school) that contributed the money to purchase the jeep for the Army.

A jeep and a 57 mm anti-tank gun prepared to be ferried across the River at Eygelehoven, the Netherlands, on 19 February 1945. It took a real need or a fertile imagination to develop this technique.

SOME VERY INTERESTING DATES

Here are some helpful dates regarding changes in the production of standardized WWII jeeps taken from an Ordnance Department report issued late in the war. The dates shown indicate month/day/year.

TRUCK, ¼ TON, 4x4 (1 Aug. 1942 to 30 Sept. 1944)
a. The Truck, ¼ Ton, 4x4, is one of the vehicles developed and procured by the Quartermaster Corps, and transferred to the Ordnance Department by direction of War Department Circular 245, and standardized by OCM item 19107 (dated 23 October 1942). Design and development of this truck was essentially complete when taken over by Ordnance.
b. Originally developed as a light reconnaissance and personnel carrier, mobile machine gun mount, and as a substitute for the motorcycle with side car and tricycle, this vehicle has become the standard truck in the ¼ ton capacity range, and has been adapted to many special operating purposes, such as wire reel cart and letter carrier.
c. Originally Bantam, Ford and Willys-Overland produced experimental lots of these vehicles for field service tests. As a result of these tests, specifications were revised and Willys-Overland produced the first large quantity production order. Subsequently, a Ford version of the Willys vehicle entered production, a duplicate of the Willys Model except in features which did not affect spare parts interchangeability between vehicles of th Ford and Willys makes. At the present time, both Ford and Willys-Overland are producing this vehicle.
d. Principal features of the Truck, ¼ ton, 4x4, are its 134 cu. in. displacement engine Ford Model GPW and Willys Model 442--identical except for minor manufacturing differences not affecting service part interchangeability, Warner Model T-84 transmission, Spicer Model 18 transfer case, front and rear axles Spicer Models 25 front and 23 rear in the Willys make, and Ford Models GPW in the Ford make vehicles--the Ford axles being duplicates of the Spicer products, combat wheels and 6.00x16 single front and rear tires.
e. Major changes made subsequent to the transfer of this vehicle to Ordnance with dates of release for production, and other items of interest, are as follows:
(1) Added guard in left tool compartment, to prevent trailer lighting socket being damaged by careless stowage of tools. 9/2/42.
(2) Relocated oil filler and drain holes on opposite side of transmission, to improve accessibility. 9/15/42.
(3) Reinforced body rear panel to prevent breakage caused by vibration of spare tire bracket in operations crosscountry. 10/22/42.
(4) Rustproofed valve springs. 1/14/43.
(5) Reinforced engine front plate, to prevent engine shifting in operations over hazardous terrain. 1/16/43.
(6) Added liquid container bracket on body rear panel, to permit carrying 5-gallon liquid container. 3/9/43.
(7) Added radio terminal box. 3/12/43.
(8) Increased section at pivot pin boss on drag link bell crank, to eliminate operating failures. 6/3/43.
(9) Eliminated blanket compartment in seat cushions as blankets were not being stowed therein, and increased thickness of cushion to improve riding comfort. 7/3/43.
(10) Added support under spare tire, to relieve body rear panel of shock loads imposed by the spare tire in operations over rough terrain. 8/12/43.
(11) Added metal shields at each side of radiator core, to prevent recirculation of hot air and improve cooling. 11/13/43.
(12) Substituted 8x1 ¾" internal expanding hand brake for 6x2" brake, to improve brake efficiency and life. 3/13/44.
(13) Added seal at lower end of hand

brake cable tube, to prevent entrance of mud. 4/10/44.

(14) Added positive seal between transmission and transfer case, to prevent interchange of lubricant between the two units. 5/30/44.

(15) Adopted heavy type chassis springs, to minimize operating failures. 6/28/44.

(16) Raised transmission lubricant level 1", to reduce oil operating temperatures. 7/10/44.

(17) Added gusset at rear of frame, to prevent cracking in hazardous operations. 7/15/44.

(18) Substituted sintered filter in fuel tank for auxiliary fuel filter in engine compartment, to minimize possibility of vapor lock, and eliminate necessity for having to service filter. 7/17/44.

(19) Relocated muffler to rear of rear axle and up under body, to afford greater protection in operations through deep mud and over rough terrain. 7/20/44.

(20) Produced 12-volt conversion kits, for 12-volt radio operation, and for limited distribution to the field. (OCM 21445 dated 24 August 1943)

(21) Produced capstan winch kit for limited distribution to field. (OCM 27944 dated 31 August 1944)

(22) Produced tandem hitch kit to make available an airborne prime mover for the 105 MM Howitzer in the form of two ¼ ton 4x4 trucks hitched together to make one prime mover. (OCM 19549 dated 2 January 1943)

f. Changes listed in paragraph e preceding, and dates on which releases for production were made, involve Willys vehicle production. Promptly after Willys-Overland is authorized to incorporate a change in production Ford duplicates the change; this as Willys-Overland maintains custody of the master drawings.

A 101st Airborne lineman repairs communication lines damaged by the heaviest snowfall in years near Haguenau, France on 20 January 1945. A jeep saved the day again.

WAR PAINT

It would not be difficult to fill a book this size with all the speculation that I've seen in print over the last 10 years about the "perfect color match" for WWII jeep paint. The subject is moot as there is no perfect color match *except the one that pleases the vehicle owner*.

When dismantling a vehicle it is often possible to find a good original swatch of 50 year old paint under a bracket or in some other out-of-the-way spot. I've looked at many of these swatches and they are nearly all different to some degree.

The US Government did specify the color of paint to be applied to their contract vehicles and for the most part the paint was applied in the manner specified. There were however, many subtleties of manufacture, preparation, environment, application and use which altered the color of the paint.

The factors below (to name just a few) can alter the color, hue and/or value of what began life as the "same color" of paint.

A. Amount of "flattener" used to make paint dull.
B. Base color over which paint was applied.
C. Humidity on the day the paint was applied.
D. Amount of thinner in paint.
E. Technique of the painter.
F. Lighting under which paint is examined.
G. Stains on paint.
H. Exposure to sunlight.

The paint chips duplicated at the right are samples of those supplied by Ditzler Automotive Finishes, a part of PPG Industries, Inc. of Troy MI USA. They made much of the paint originally used on WWII era MBs and GPWs. While they can be a useful reference, even the process of printing the colors on the paper of this book *can* alter the colors somewhat. The numbers under the colors are Ditzler numbers.

NOTES REGARDING THE PAINTING OF MARKINGS ON MILITARY VEHICLES

By looking at war-time photos alone it becomes obvious that the people who put stars, letters, numbers, etc. on jeeps WERE NOT students of Army Regulation 850-5, which prescribed the placement of such marks on various vehicles.

One can find extreme off-the-wall examples of every inconsistency imaginable. An article in the program for the 11th convention of the MVCC, written by member Ed Girroir sheds a lot of light on why there were so many inconsistencies and why the markings were so poorly done.

Girroir served in France and Germany as a member of the crew of an M8 Armored Car. He mentioned the painting of markings and went on to explain:

"When we first were issued our vehicles, they needed to have all the markings; stars, numbers, etc. applied. It is interesting to hear some restorers remark about how the star for example should be exactly 5 inches from some reference point on the vehicle. The truth is that when the markings were added, two factors applied more than any others. First, we were in a hurry: lay the template down and spray it. If it oversprays, so what. Second, the Sergeant who was usually in charge, would find someone who had done something not to the Sergeant's liking, and painting was a punishment. Therefore, the Sarge would make it as difficult as he wished for the lowly GI putting the markings on. He would require that the stars for example be put in the most out of the way places, just to be mean and teach that GI a lesson. So vehicle marking, especially in combat areas, was very much up to the old Sarge."

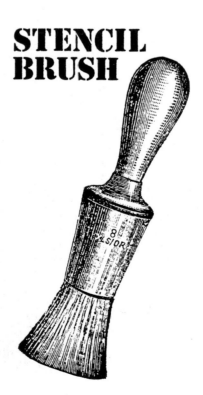

STENCIL BRUSH

Color	Number
Marking White	8282
Nameplate Red	71662
Nameplate Green	43723
Marking Blue	13598
USMC Marking	81958
Navy Gray	32353
Ford Gray	32908
Army OD	40973
USMC OD	40458
Accessory Black	9000/9300

OIL FILLER TUBES AND DIPSTICKS

(see facing page)

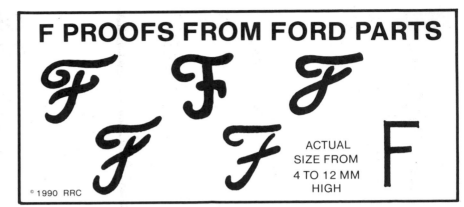
The fact that so few jeeps survive with their original engine intact is not so much a commentary on the durability of the Go-Devil as it is on inadequate servicing and the ridiculous expectations of those who operated them in the service. Anyone willing to spend a couple of hours in the return area of a rental car operation will get a pretty good idea of how a motor pool operates. Except that motor pools don't have to make a profit and the "renters" at motor pools don't have to pay for what they break or wreck.

By the time most jeeps were declared surplus, many had their parts intermingled with the parts of lots of other jeeps. After a few years in civilian hands, even more parts were exchanged and replaced. Little wonder then that one can find a 1942 GPW with the oil filler tube from a 1945 MB.

Because the oil filler tube and dipstick (oil level indicator) are such obvious parts on any engine, it is worth the effort to make sure that the style used on your engine matches the era of your machine. There were at least four major variations used on MBs and GPWs. Of the pre-standardized jeeps only the MA used a common oil filler tube and dipstick -- the Bantam and Ford GP having a dipstick completely separate from the oil filler tube. The MA tube and dipstick (A) may also be found on Willys car engines and on many early MB engines. It is unique that there is no flare at the top of the tube.

Style B is the first type with a flared neck, to facilitate adding oil to the engine. The cap of the dipstick fits over the outside of the flared neck. This style was used on a small number of MBs and GPWs through the fall of 1942 production.

An improved dipstick with a locking cap was introduced in late 1942 or early 1943 production (C). This cap contains a gasket which provides a good seal when locked down with a clockwise twist and a fin on top for a secure grip.

Style D is virtually the same as C except that it has a tube added to the neck to recycle crankcase vapor through the air-intake system ahead of the carburetor. This tube and dipstick were common to the MB, GPW and the CJ-2A produced after WWII,

and similar to those used on the M38 jeep. The dipsticks all indicate about 2¼ inches of oil level between the EMPTY and FULL marks (E). Some are found with graduations between EMPTY and FULL but such marks are uncommon. All the dipsticks came originally with a baffel (F) mounted on the stick about halfway between the cap and the end. Some were swaged to the stick and other types were spot-welded on (type shown). These baffels are often missing.

The purpose of the small hole drilled in the corner of one of the fins on the caps of dipsticks C and D has puzzled many collectors. Quite simply, it was there to provide a place to wire a metal tag which gave some specific information -- the weight of oil to be used, for example. The metal tags were of a peculiar sort with wavy edges and a slot in the end. This odd shape allowed them to be held in an Addressograph machine, in which the inscription was applied to the metal in the same manner as the inscription on American "dog tags" or identity discs.

A Pyrene ad from the time of WWII showing the standard MV version at the right (Fortune Magazine).

F PROOFS (ABOVE) Other variants on these logos are double-strikes and reversed or "mirror" images. Reverse images occurred when the logo die was inserted in the bolt header backwards.

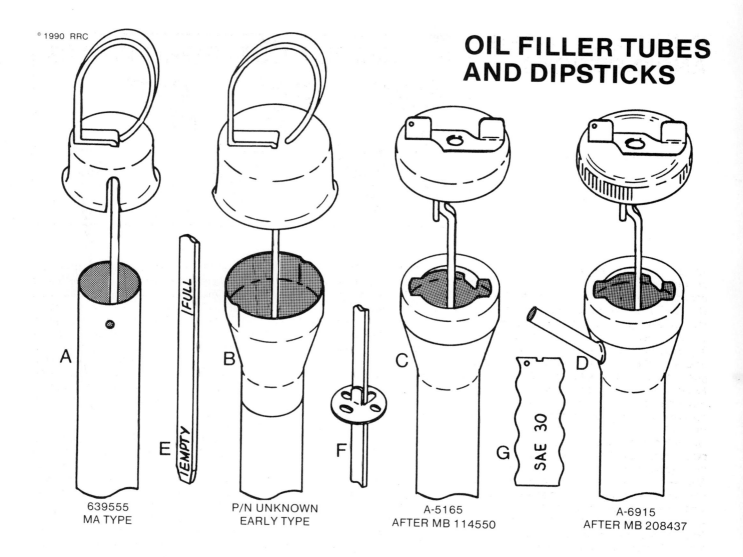

OIL FILLER TUBES AND DIPSTICKS

A — 639555 MA TYPE

B — P/N UNKNOWN EARLY TYPE

C — A-5165 AFTER MB 114550

D — A-6915 AFTER MB 208437

E — FULL / EMPTY

F

G — SAE 30

SUDDEN LOSS OF OIL PRESSURE

Because of the potential for a great deal of damage from a loss of engine oil pressure, and the current situation in which ethanol is sometimes mixed with fuel by gasoline companies, I have decided it is necessary to caution jeep owners about a special problem.

Ethanol added to gasoline makes the gasoline more profitable to sell at the pump and uses up great quantities of grain, which has been in surplus in some countries for a long time. Before adding gasoline to the tank of your jeep *always* inquire to determine if the fuel has any ethanol in it. If it contains ethanol, AVOID IT.

The damage done by ethanol is that it tends to dissolve some of the synthetic materials it comes in contact with while circulating through the fuel system. The problematic component in every jeep fuel system is the fuel pump and more particularly the fuel pump diaphragm. The synthetic fuel pump diaphragm may have functioned well for 40 years, *but it can fail* with the first tank of ethanol blended gasoline. Ethanol can turn the diaphragm to a slice of jelly. As the diaphragm turns to jelly, it perforates. It may very well continue to pump an adequate supply of fuel to the engine, but gasoline *will* leak through the holes in the diaphragm and into the crankcase. As the quantity of fuel increases in a crankcase, the oil thins out and the oil pressure drops very drastically. Naturally, this process can take minutes or days depending on the condition of the diaphragm and the concentration of ethanol in the fuel. The three obvious signs that you have a problem are dropping oil pressure, a black or sooty tailpipe and blue smoke coming from the tailpipe.

At the first indication of trouble, stop the vehicle and check the oil. Don't just check the oil level, *smell* the dipstick and the oil filler tube. If you smell gasoline, it is *very* likely that the diaphragm IS ruptured.

Gasoline is a fine solvent for removing oil so it is dangerous to drive your jeep with gas in the crankcase. Parts will wear at a very rapid rate. All this is a good reason to use STP Oil Treatment with every oil change in any valuable car -- gasoline can't remove it.

The cure for the problem is obvious. The fuel pump must be repaired or replaced and the oil must be changed. This done, the oil pressure should return to its previous reading.

The MB in this photo is serial number 437405 delivered on 01 May 1945. It belongs to Robert Dahl and is restored to the appearance of immediately after WWII.

A typical Willys-Overland MB engine as painted during the WWII era, Variances in the color scheme do occur.

A typical Ford GPW engine as painted during the WWII era. Variances in the color scheme do occur.

¼ TON TOYS

Many would argue that jeep toys have no place in a book about WWII military jeeps. That may have been true some years ago, but 50 years after the fact I can assure you they do.

The MB/GPW toys built during and just after WWII were made because jeeps were exciting, interesting vehicles. Everybody wanted a jeep and if they couldn't have one, at least they could have a toy or model. The great variety of jeep toys available in the mid-to-late 1940s are themselves a marvelous testament to the enormous popularity of the real thing.

Toy jeeps have now become quite valuable in their own right, not only among jeep restorers but among toy collectors as well. Prices for small jeeps of the 1940s can often exceed $100.00 and some of the pedal jeeps in very good condition can bring in excess of $1000.00

The jeep toys and models illustrated here are not meant to be a complete or comprehensive listing. Rather, I have attempted to depict an interesting group of rather common types, and to the extent possible identify the manufacturer. Because toy collectors also collect jeep toys one thing

can be said with certainty: the more complex and realistic any model of a jeep is, the more valuable it is. Models of large size (12 inches, 30 cm long or more) and those which come with their original package are especially desirable.

As a category of collectible toys, jeeps are still (1990) a bargain. I can predict that as jeep people (rather than toy people) begin to collect jeep toys, and as toy people start to recognize how many of "us" there are the prices will escalate sharply. If you wish to assemble a collection of toy jeeps of WWII period the time to do it is now.

ID model of the ¼ ton truck as made for the US Government during WWII by Dale Model Co of Chicago. If you decide you are going to have just one model of a jeep, this is the one you should look for. If you find one with two of the wheels missing, buy it anyway. When you do find an ID jeep with four wheels the spare will be missing as it is held in place with a screw. These were sold surplus after the war as cheap sandbox toys.

ID JEEP

The single most important toy jeep of the WWII era is the US Government identification model of the famous ¼ ton. Most people know the government made black plastic models of Allied and enemy aircraft during the war, but few are aware of the vehicle models they made. Unlike the aircraft, the vehicles are hollow-cast from metal and they are quite heavy. The proportions are excellent and the detailing is quite good. All I have seen were originally painted olive drab.

The purpose of the ID models was of course, to train soldiers to visually differentiate between Allied and Axis vehicles at a glance. It was extremely important for gunners to be able to tell the difference because in many circumstances it was necessary to identify a target and fire at it in a split-second. In spite of all the intensive training in this sort of thing the history of WWII is filled with incidents of Allied and Axis soldiers and pilots firing on their own planes and vehicles.

The ID model of the MB/GPW is 5 ½ inches (140 mm) long and weighs 14

ounces (400 g). It comes with 5 separately cast wheels and on the spare is the name of the company that made it - *Dale Model Co. Chicago*. The windshield is cast in the down position and a star in a circle is visible centered on the cowl. In the center of the bottom behind the rear axle is the word JEEP. I have seen good jeep ID models bring $100.00 and have bought some myself for as little as $7.50. My experience has been that sellers usually ask more for the US vehicles than the German or Japanese vehicles, probably because the US vehicles look more familiar. Many of the vehicles other than the jeep were built by *COMETAL*.

This is a view of the rear and right side of the US ID model of the MB/GPW.

The bottom of the same jeep by Dale Model Co. showing the hollow-cast form.

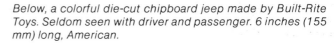

Above is a jeep sawed from a solid block of wood with a bent wire windshield and a very heavy canvas top. 6 ½ inches (170 mm) long, probably European.

Below, a commercial wooden model of a MA with composition wheels. It must have been one of the first packaged models of the jeep. 5 ¼ inches (135 mm), American.

Above, a finely detailed small sheet metal model of a jeep probably made in the Netherlands just after the war. 4 ¾ inches (125 mm) long.

Below, a colorful die-cut chipboard jeep made by Built-Rite Toys. Seldom seen with driver and passenger. 6 inches (155 mm) long, American.

The jeep in the foreground of this picture is GPW 65685 delivered on 12 August 1942. It belongs to Merrill Madsen and carries the markings of VMF-212 as used in the period of 1944-1952. The one in the back is MB 201878 delivered on 01 November 1942. It

belongs to Ray Cowdery and carries the markings of VMF-214, typical of the WWII period. VMF is the USMC abbreviation for heavier-than-air (V) Marine fighter squadron (MF).

Here are a couple of the best European versions of the toy jeep that were sold widely in America. Above, the Arnold from West Germany is a 6 ¾ inch (170 mm) long, steerable, sheet metal unit that came with removable figures and a fold-down windshield. Lines Brothers, Limited of London made the Tri-Ang Minic clockwork jeep shown with its beautiful box in the photo below. 6 ¼ inches (160 mm) long. Many of the toys shown in this section are from the collection of Brian Cowdery.

Above is one of the biggest selling post-war toy jeeps, made in many variations and paint schemes by Marx Toys. A towable trailer and an artillery piece that fired wooden bullets were available as accessories. 11 ¾ inches (300 mm) long, American.

In the upper-right is a two seat version of the jeep in cast aluminum by Al-Toy (Toledo Brass). It rides on rubber tires with WILLYS spaced around the metal hubcaps. An engine is cast in place under the hinged hood. 11 inches (280 mm) long, American.

Right (above) is a clear glass jeep originally made as a candy container. It came with a chipboard cover on the bottom. 4 ¼ inches (110 mm) long, American.

Right (below) is a crude commercial wooden model of the ¼ ton from the time of WWII. 5 inches (130 mm) long, American.

In the lower-right corner is a very well made stamped metal jeep with a wind-up drive. It came with a driver and passengers. 4 ¾ inches (125 mm) long, marked MADE IN US ZONE GERMANY.

Below, a stamped metal jeep toy with a wind-up drive. Has a French regimental insigne on the hood. 5 inches (130 mm) long, French (?)

Here's a photo of WWII US vehicle ID models to give you an idea of the range available. Tanks and halftracks with turrets that turn are rare as they were easily broken.

The MB shown here is restored to WWII Navy configuration with markings of Motor Torpedo Squadron 33. It is MB number 196380 delivered 16 December 1942 and is owned by Steve Greenberg.

This view of a capstan winch shows the capstan, the data plate and the Ford mounting of the unit (see also page 211).
NOTE: Sockets behind bumper gussets are flag holders.

This MB number 121060 was delivered 26 February 1942 and carries the markings of the 505 Military Police Section. Owned by Reg Hodgson and Jim Fitzgerald.

Above is the box (unbuilt model and glue still inside) for the West-Craft die-cut kit model of the jeep. This one is scaled at 1 inch = 1 foot like the Marx and the Al-Toy. Dated 1943, American.

Left, an extremely rare paperweight made of fine brown composition material and depicting three GIs in pre-war helmets riding in a prototype jeep. The reverse side has the identical image. 3 ¾ inches (95 mm) wide.

A selection of the beautiful but tiny jeep models currently made by Jiri Trnka are shown in these 3 photos. Even the tiniest details are faithfully preserved. Trnkas' address is Drevarska ul. 8, CZ-602 00 Brno, Czechoslovakia. Photos by L. Kulka.

JEEP ROPE

The photo shows a rope of the proper size with the right kind of eyes correctly wrapped on the front bumper of a MB. The rope is one inch (25 mm) in diameter and 12 feet (3.66 m) long overall. The eyes on each end are about one foot (30 cm) long. One eye is slipped over the bumper and the rope is wrapped as far as it will go. The other eye then goes over the remaining bumper end and is wired to the bumper gusset.

SPLICING AN EYE ON A ROPE

To make an eye at the end of the rope follow these instructions and the diagrams A-G on this page. It is a simple process if you simply do it step-by-step.

A) Untwist about eight inches (20 cm) of the end of the rope so you have three separate strands, or smaller sections of rope. Make a loop about one foot (30 cm) long and lay two loose strands *over* the triple (main) rope and one loose strand *under* it.

B) Put the number 2 strand end under any one of the strands in the main rope and pull it up snug.

C) Put the number 1 strand end under the strand of the main rope *just above* the one the number 2 strand went under. Pull it up snug.

D) Turn the partly formed eye over and notice there is *one* strand of the main rope *without* a strand under it. Put the number 3 strand under this unused one and pull it up snug and make sure it is pointing the same direction around the main rope as the other two are.

At this point look over your work to see that the strands sticking out of the main rope are all about the same length and that the eye is the size you want it. The tension on all three strands should be the same and the junction of the end strands and the main rope should be tight.

E, F, G) Continue the process in the manner started of putting a strand end *over* a single strand of the main rope and *under* the next strand above. Keep the tension snug on each strand as you pull them under the strands of the main rope. When you run out of loose ends to entwine with the main rope the splice is finished and so is the eye.

Any excess length of single strand may be cut off with a sharp knife so they don't stick out from the rope like those in illustration G. Lay the eye on the floor and roll the splice back and forth under your foot and it will taper out nicely. Now do it all over again on the other end of the rope.

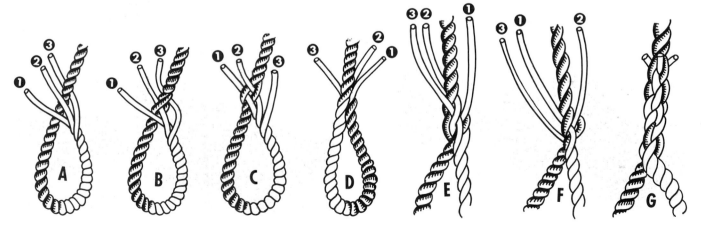

239

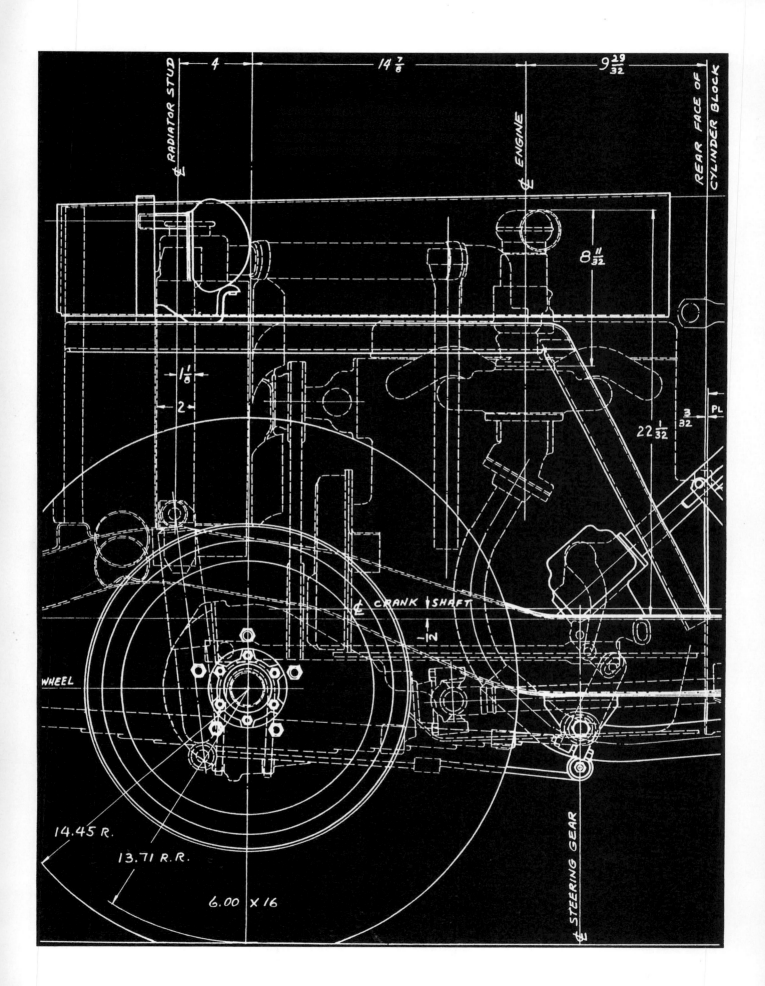

JERRICANS

The American jerrican (Jerry = German + can) was as the name implies, adapted from a similar can used by the German Army in Africa. British military units had captured samples of the German 20 liter variety and had forwarded them to the Office of the US Quartermaster General for evaluation in the summer of 1940.

A subsequent report from the Armed Forces Board found the Wehrmacht cans to be stackable, strong and light, useful with any fluid, to have an excellent handle and spout and that no accessories were needed for use. The Motor Transport Division of the Quartermaster Corps endorsed the can and ordered their Depot at Camp Holabird, Maryland, to draw up specifications for an American version.

It was found that the German can was designed to be built from a few easily stamped parts in small shops and in rather small numbers. A decision was made to redesign parts of the can to make it easier to manufacture on American assembly lines in large quantity and to make it a five US gallon can. The changes involved altering the design from a can of two somewhat similar pieces welded along a center seam to a can made of three main sec-

tions with welded seams and a rolled-on bottom. The cam style closure was abandoned in favor of the Army standard 2 ½ inch threaded top found on the old US ten gallon container. In the end there was one feature that was common to both the US and German can - a three-bar handle on top that made it easy to pass the can from man-to-man.

By Autumn 1940 the US Quartermaster Corps had advertised for bids and awarded contracts to four firms for the new five gallon can. The first four makers were: Chattanooga Stamping Company, National Enameling and Stamping Company, Pittsburgh Steel Barrel Company, and Wheeling Corrugating Company. Production figures are not available for 1941 and 1942 but they were high enough so that every Ford and Willys jeep produced after 1 August 1942 (MB serial number 165582) came with a spare gas can attached to the rear panel. During 1943, 1944 and 1945 22,443,000 US pattern cans were produced, 2,528,944 of them at a US Army-owned plant in Great Britain operated by Magnatex, Ltd.

Very shortly after the D-Day landings in Normandy (6 June 1944) a severe short-

age of US five gallon spare fuel cans developed throughout Allied units in Europe. The shortage was cured by the shipment of millions of British jerricans which were nearly identical to the German Wehrmacht twenty liter can with the cam lock spout.

By comparison, the German/British style can weighed 11 ½ pounds empty and 44 pounds full while the American can weighed 10 pounds empty and 40 pounds when full. The "tin can" type construction of the US version proved to be ideal for a high-volume product and less that 1% of American production was found to leak.

A spout nearly identical to the German/ British cam lock spout was tried on cans made for the US Marine Corps in 1943 and was deemed satisfactory after testing.

A five gallon US pattern water can was put into production in the summer of 1942. It was the same size and of similar construction to the gas can except for the spout and the baked-on synthetic lining. The 3 ½ inch cam lock spout made the can easier to clean inside after it had been used for food (soup or coffee, for example) and the lining prevented rust.

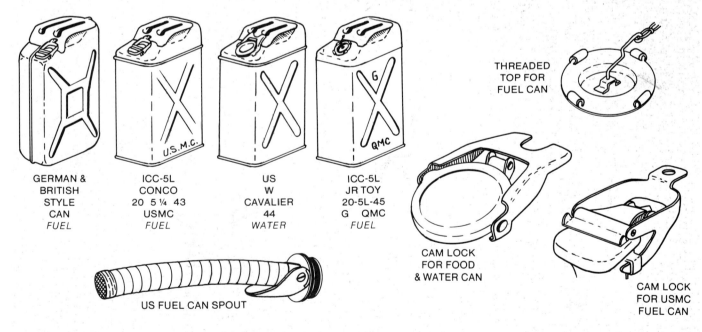

GERMAN &
BRITISH
STYLE
CAN
FUEL

ICC-5L
CONCO
20 5 ¼ 43
USMC
FUEL

US
W
CAVALIER
44
WATER

ICC-5L
JR TOY
20-5L-45
G   QMC
FUEL

THREADED
TOP FOR
FUEL CAN

CAM LOCK
FOR FOOD
& WATER CAN

CAM LOCK
FOR USMC
FUEL CAN

US FUEL CAN SPOUT

1941-1945
US 5 Gallon Spare Gas Can and
US 5 Gallon Water Can Production

	1941	1942	1943	1944	1945	TOTAL
WATER	?	1,830,000	1,265,000	2,951,000	598,000	6,644,000
GAS	?	?	14,291,000	4,157,000	3,995,000	22,443,000

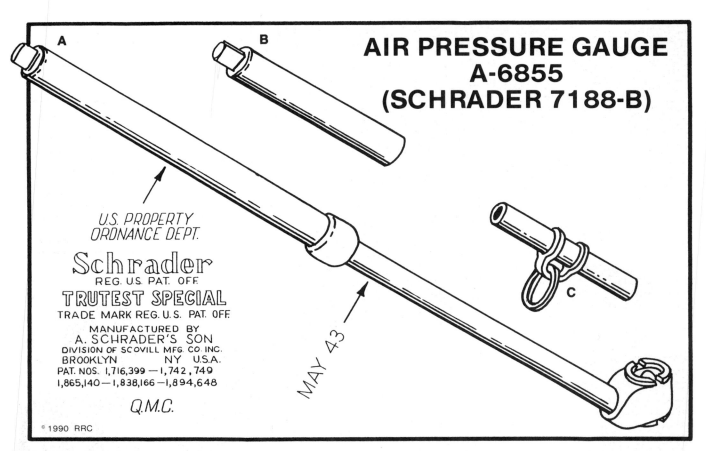

AIR PRESSURE GAUGE
A-6855
(SCHRADER 7188-B)

U.S. PROPERTY
ORDNANCE DEPT.

Schrader
REG. U.S. PAT. OFF.

TRUTEST SPECIAL
TRADE MARK REG. U.S. PAT. OFF.

MANUFACTURED BY
A. SCHRADER'S SON
DIVISION OF SCOVILL MFG. CO. INC.
BROOKLYN   NY   U.S.A.
PAT. NOS. 1,716,399 — 1,742,749
1,865,140 — 1,838,166 — 1,894,648

Q.M.C.

© 1990 RRC

This illustration shows a typical brass dual-foot hand gauge as furnished with MBs and GPWs. The information stamped on the tube is shown below the picture. Type A has a flat indicator while type B has a square one. C shows a hanging ring sometimes found on the small diameter tube.

This Willys-Overland ad from very early in 1942 is an excellent example of the kind of "puffery" that got them in so much trouble with the US Federal Trade Commission. Willys was required by the FTC to refrain from their claims that they had invented the "jeep".

TM 31-200, Maintenance and Care of Pneumatic Tires and Rubber Treads (20 April 1942) shows these four tire valve caps as being commonly used on US military vehicles. B and D of course have forked ends to facilitate removal of valve cores.

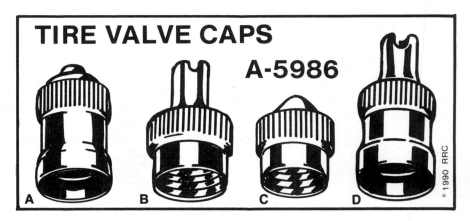

TIRE VALVE CAPS
A-5986

A   B   C   D

© 1990 RRC

The Jeep calls them Daddy...

THE QUARTERMASTER CORPS OF THE U. S. ARMY AND THE CIVILIAN ENGINEERS OF WILLYS-OVERLAND

We pay public tribute here, to the Engineers of Willys—the most highly lauded automotive engineering staff that the pressure and inspiration of war have brought to light.

These are the men whose engineering skill and creative minds, added to those of the Quartermaster Corps of the U. S. Army, gave birth to the amazing Jeep of today. No other single mobile unit is so typical of modern mechanized war.

And it *proves*, beyond question, that the Willys Go-Devil *Engine* and the defense-time Willys *American* were no "door step" babies, but legitimate offspring of fine engineering practice that is both fundamentally sound and reliable. Willys-Overland Motors, Inc.

TODAY do your part. Conserve rubber and other materials vital to war equipment. Buy defense stamps and bonds. Pay taxes with a smile. Whatever the total price you pay, it will be as nothing compared to the value of continued Freedom. . . . . . TOMORROW, make your first new post-war car a Willys—"The Jeep in Civvies."

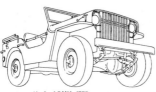

U. S. ARMY JEEP

WILLYS

MOTOR CARS   TRUCKS AND JEEPS

AMERICAR
the People's Car

THE GO-DEVIL ENGINE—power-heart of WILLYS CARS and all JEEPS

Strange as it may seem now, it was only a few years ago (the illustration at the right is from the mid 1970s) when anybody who needed parts for an old MB or GPW could just order them from Sears-Roebuck & Company. America's largest retailer continued to produce and mail a special 44 page catalog containing virtually every jeep part and accessory until nearly 1980. Carburetors at $21.75, short blocks at $242.00 and NOS Speedometers at $24.25 would have been great investments if you had paid retail at Sears and just stashed them away.

When Sears dropped out, other entrepreneurs got in, and MB/GPW lovers are fortunate that there is good availability of NOS, reproduction and used parts for the restoration of old ¼ tons. Listed below are many firms that supply parts for old jeeps. Some carry a full line while others specialize in certain categories of parts. Some have catalogs you can purchase while others do not. If these people do not have the parts you are after they can often help you find a source.

REPLACEMENT PARTS FOR WWII JEEPS

NEW CARBURETORS and Repair Accessories

Sears

(3 and 4) Make your own carburetor repairs. Each kit contains all necessary parts for repairing carburetor, dual or single as indicated.

IMPORTANT: To order state F28 LM 1000V, then kit number. One needed per model

Item	Model Number	Part Number	Shpg. wt.	Price
(3) Single Carburetor Repair Kit	MB.	119042	(6 oz.)	$18.20
	M38.	648065	(4 oz.)	13.20
	M38A1.	807885	(6 oz.)	12.98
	CJ2A, CJ3A.	647745	(4 oz.)	13.75
	CJ3B, CJ5 (4-cyl.), CJ6 (4-cyl.)*	924160	(4 oz.)	7.25
	CJ5 (V6), CJ6 (V6)	7016448	(6 oz.)	9.50
	C101 (V6)	940772	(6 oz.)	1.33
(4) Dual Carburetor Repair Kit	CJ5 (V6), CJ6 (V6) with Rochester carb. 7026086 only.	7016632	(6 oz.)	9.95
	C101(V6), CJ5(V6), CJ6 (V6) with Rochester carb. 7026082	7016655	(6 oz.)	11.05

*With Carter Carb. YF4002S use kit 940772.

Choppy acceleration, rough idle and poor gas mileage may be the result of a faulty carburetor. Help pep up acceleration, reduce gas consumption and improve engine performance with an all-new carburetor from Sears. Manufactured by well-known carburetor makers, each carburetor meets or exceeds original equipment specifications. Analyzer-tested for proper air and fuel mixture.

IMPORTANT: State F28LM1000V, then part number.

Item	Model Number	Part Number	Shpg. wt.	Price
Single Carb Assembly	MB.	647844	4 lbs.	$21.75
	M38.	A17854	8 lbs.	32.95
	M38A1.	804826	6 lbs.	39.20
	CJ2A, CJ3A.	923806	4 lbs.	36.95
	CJ3B, CJ5 (4-cyl.)▲, CJ6 (4-cyl.)▲	923808	5 lbs.	29.98
	CJ5 (V6), CJ6 (V6).	7016507	7 lbs.	29.65
	C101 (4-cylinder)	943193	5 lbs.	26.89
Dual Carb	CJ5 (V6), CJ6 (V6).	941343	6 lbs.	33.50
	C101 (V6)	943187	6 lbs.	36.95

▲Late models with Carter carb. YF40025 use 943193.

ANTELOPE VALLEY EQUIPMENT
AND TRUCK PARTS
44532 Trevor
Lancaster, CA 93534

ARMY JEEP PARTS
P.O. Box 1006
Canal & Jefferson Sts., Annex
Bristol, PA 19007 USA

ATLANTIC AUTOMOTIVE LIMITED
Pattenden Lane
Marden, Nr. Tonbridge
Kent TN12 9QS
United Kingdom

BACCHI MARIA
Via Bazzanese 32
I - 40033 Casalecchio Reno
Bologna
Italy

BEACHWOOD CANVAS WORKS
P.O. Box 137
Island Heights, NJ 08732 USA

DIRECT SUPPORT
P.O. Box 317
Pittsfield, MA 01202 USA

DIVISION ORDNANCE
Box 206
Stephens City, VA 22655 USA

WAYNE DOWDLE
2896 Walnut Gr. Rd.
Memphis, TN 38111 USA

4WD BY VAN
24000 Ventura Blvd.
Calabasas, CA 91302 USA

FORNITURE TESSILI NAVALI
Via Vicolo alla Vigna
I - 22070 Capiago (Como)
Italy

PER HOGAN PARTS-ACCESSORIES
Marjdalsvejen 30
N - Oslo 1
Norway

I.I.T. - TAMARRI ANDREA
via Fratelli Cervi 5/A
I - 40129 Bologna
Italy

J.D.E.S.
Meierhofstrasse 24
CH - 8820 Waedenswil
Switzerland

JEEPACRES
Rt. 1, Box 237
New Carlisle, IN 46552 USA

JEEP JUNK
117 Van Dyke Dr.
Canton, IL 61520 USA

MIDTJYDSK, RESERVE DELSLAGER
Fanovej 9
DK - Viborg 8800
Denmark

MILITARY PATTERN VEHICLES
R.R. 2
Beamsville
Ontario L0R 1B0
Canada

MILITARY VEHICLE PARTS CO.
1425 Friendly Woods Rd.
Blythewood, SC 29016 USA

DARCY F. MILLER
15 Farhall Place
Glenhaven
New South Wales 2153
Australia

MISC INC.
7-6-5 Kamirenjaku
Mitaka-shi, Tokyo
181 Japan

BRENT MULLINS JEEP PARTS
P.O. Box 9599
College Station, TX 77842 USA

MURRAY JEEP PARTS
Box 214
Dover, DE 19903 USA

NELSON'S SURPLUS JEEPS
1024 East Park Ave.
Columbiana, OH 44408 USA

NORTHERN PARTS & SUPPLY
Box, 477, Route 11
No. Bangor, NY 12966 USA

R.E.O.M.I.E. b.v.
Erlecomsedam 30
P.O. Box 10
NL - 6576 JW OOY
The Netherlands

RI.MA.FER S.A.S.
Via Emilia Ovest 386
I - 41100 Modena
Italy

RAPCO/FORT RYAN SUPPLY
Mark Dodd
P.O. Box 191
Bowie, TX 76230 USA

SARAFAN AUTO SUPPLY
Box 293
Spring Valley, NY 10977 USA

MIKE SCHOLER
Box 2019
Riverview, FL 33569 USA

SURPLUS CITY JEEP PARTS
11794 Sheldon St.
Sun Valley, CA 91352 USA

M. VAN DE VELDE & CO. S.P.R.L.
Chaussee de Bruxelles, 14
B - 1474 Ways
Belgium

WILLIAM WARREN
107 Westside Blvd.
Newton, NC 28658 USA

WHITE OWL PARTS
3201 W. Vernon Ave.
Kinston, NC 28501 USA

WILLYS MPLS
301 Pine Street
Farmington, MN 55024 USA

WILLYS WORKS
1933 West Gardner Lane
Tuscon, AZ 85705 USA

"Welcome to the jeeps" or "Bienvenue aux jeeps". One of the most symbolic pictures of the WWII jeep is the shot below. It is one of a series of the photo postcards by Photo-Presse-Liberation and shows French ladies giving flowers to their liberators.

LOCK, GLOVE BOX A-3532

The first jeeps came without a glovebox on the right side of the dash. At MB number 120,698 a locking glovebox door was added. Because the lock contained a bolt that rose and fell with the turning of a H700 key, a semicircular spring was affixed at the hinge which was intended to keep the door closed even if the bolt was not raised. (The bolt when raised fitted into a slot punched in the upper rim of the glovebox). The closing spring often got lost or failed, so a keyless push-button door lock replaced the keyed type from MB 134,356 and the semicircular spring was eliminated. The keyless lock had a push-button that when depressed disengaged a spring-loaded locking dog from a striker plate screwed to the inside of the dash. The difference between the two types is obvious even with the glovebox closed if one looks for the striker plate screw on the later model.

As the keyed lock appeared on only 13,658 MB jeeps (it was also used by Ford) they are not common. Great care must be taken in removing the keyed lock and there is a trick to getting the bolt out of the back of the lock so you can take off the nut and dismount the lock. Here it is:

Turn the key *counter* clock-wise to lower the bolt. Open the door and grasp the bolt with the thumb and forefinger of the left hand. Pull out (away from the door) on the bottom of the bolt and *at the same time* turn the key another ⅛ of a turn counter-clockwise with the right hand AND PULL ON THE KEY.

The cylinder *and* the key will come out of the knob. At this point the bolt can be lifted out the top of the lock body and the nut can be removed.

BOLT

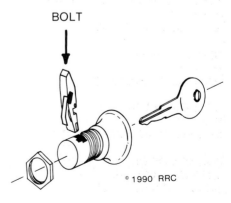

© 1990 RRC

THE READERS OF VOLUME I OF AAW ASKED FOR . . . .

Pictures of the principal types of pintle hooks used on WWII era jeeps. There is, of course, style 1 depicted here which is sort of a generic cast steel pintle hook found on most Willys MB ¼ tons. It is W-O part number A-593 and many were made by Holland Hitch Company. The first type had no chain eyes for trailer safety chains. They were an afterthought added after MB 158372 in July 1942.

Style 2 is just the Ford version of the Willys pintle hook, part number GPW 5182. The biggest difference is that the Ford pintle hook has a big script F cast right on it.

The 3rd style shown here is a late-war innovation - a pintle hook made up of pieces of stamped steel. A very classy touch on any Late Production jeep.

Style 4 is shown here for reference only. It is a pintle hook from a M series vehicle, like a M38. It has zerk fittings on it and should be used on a WWII vintage jeep *only* until you find a correct one.

❶ **❷**

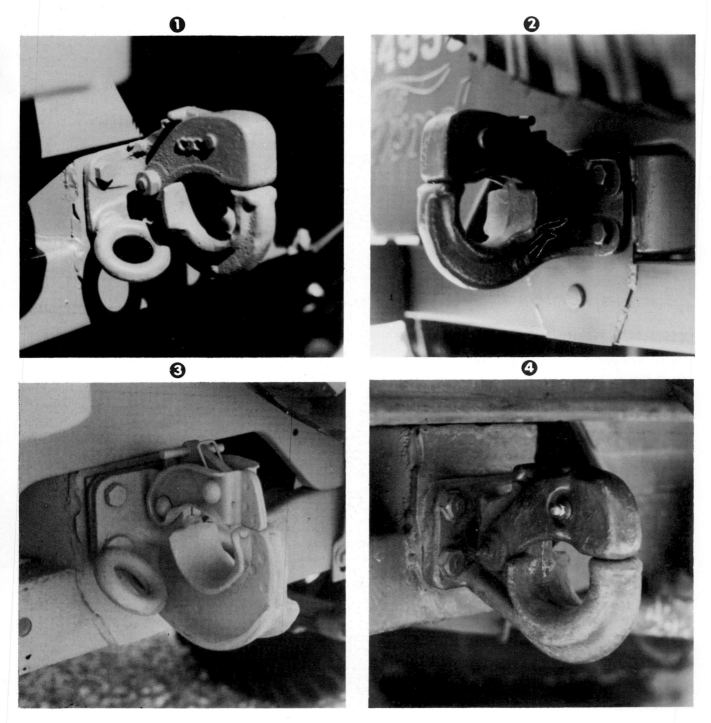

❸ **❹**

Pictures of parts for MBs and GPWs in the *original Government packages* so they would know what to look for. The Ford coil (lower left) and the Willys tail light (lower right) are almost recognizable in their paraffin and paper wrappings. Parts in boxes were also dipped in waterproofing after the lables were applied. The wiring harness in the center has a Ford Motor Company tag wired to it.

Photos exist showing Very Early Production MBs and GPWs *without* the manufacturers name on the rear panel.

❶

Pictures of Ford and Willys script on the rear panel of VEP jeeps. The photos show not only the names but also the rubber tail light grommet, pintle hooks *without* chain eyes and the round base reflex reflector assemblies that are correct features for VEP ¼ tons. Please note that the reflectors are held in place with ¼" - 28 x ½" round head screws, *not* hex head bolts.

Brigadier General Lewis Pick directed much of the work on the Burma Road (Pick's Pike) and he is seen here standing in the lead vehicle of the first convoy from India to Kumming, China.

Filipinos help land a GPW on Panay Island on 18 March 1945. Tire chains and a tall but unconventional air intake couldn't get the job done alone.

TANDEM TRAILER KIT

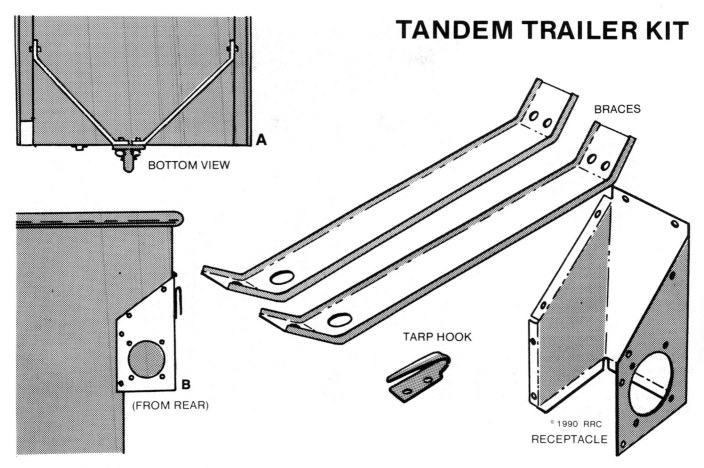

BRACES

A

BOTTOM VIEW

B

(FROM REAR)

TARP HOOK

© 1990 RRC

RECEPTACLE

The versatility of the jeep amazed those who used it and as the war progressed the equipment it carried and pulled was modified and added to in an effort to get the most from the machine. An interesting adaptation was a kit that was *not* added to the jeep itself, but to a trailer pulled by a jeep. By installing the tandem trailer kit to a towed trailer, a second trailer could be coupled to the first one doubling the towed load.

The kit was simple. It consisted of two 45° braces, a 3-sided metal box used as the receptacle for an electrical coupling socket, a coupling socket, a tarpaulin rope hook, a pintle hook and eyes, wiring and clips and an assortment of fasteners and washers to attach the parts to the rear of the first towed trailer.

The braces were bolted inside the side rails and at the center of the rear cross-member, where they supported the mount-

ing of the new pintle hook (see drawing A). The coupling socket receptacle was attached to the upper right rear corner of the trailer box (drawing B) and was wired to accept the coupling socket cable from the second towed trailer. The receptacle when installed covered the right rear tarp rope hook (welded on) so a spare was included to be bolted to the face of the receptacle itself. AWdB

Ford rear seat mounting brackets have a logo F stamped on the back of the loop. They are also obvious at a glance because of the heavy material they were made from.

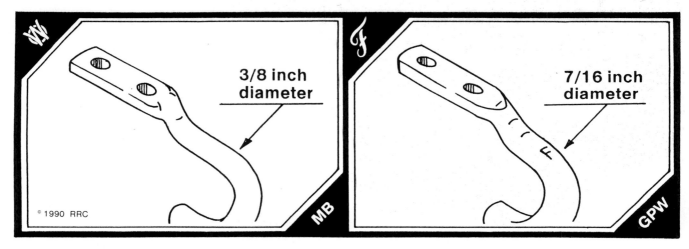

3/8 inch diameter

MB

© 1990 RRC

7/16 inch diameter

F

GPW

DATA PLATE AND FIRST AID KIT BRACKET DASHBOARD MOUNTING TEMPLATE

PHOTOCOPY AND TAPE TO DASHBOARD TO CENTER - PUNCH FOR HOLES.

3⅜ INCHES
85 MM
TO EDGE OF TEMPERATURE GAUGE HOLE

FIRST AID KIT BRACKET MOUNTS HERE ON INSIDE OF DASHBOARD WITH 3/16 x 3/8 INCH BOLTS

TRAILER TOWING DATA PLATE MOUNTS HERE WITH SHEET METAL SCREWS OR DRIVE RIVETS

BOTTOM LINE OF DASHBOARD

FINDING PARTS IN MV MANUALS

Military parts lists can be a little hard to use at times, and that's understandable if you realize they were written in a hurry and by a committee. Everybody had a different idea about where within the manual, a part should be located.

There is a simple twist in thinking that will often make it easier to locate problem parts: Rule #1 is LOOK FOR THE ATTACHING PARTS (usually bolts and nuts) THAT HOLD THE ITEM YOU SEEK IN PLACE ON THE VEHICLE and *they* will direct you to the part. Here is an example:

Many people have found 6 extra holes across the front of an MB hood *in addi-* tion to the 4 holes required for mounting the windshield bumpers. As there was nothing attached through the holes when they got their jeep where should they start looking and what should they look for?

Start with a good manual - the *TM-10-1186 Willys Master Parts List for Trucks and Trailers.* On Page 134 in Government Group 1704 one will find a listing for all (?) the parts for the *Hood.* Well, most of the parts anyway. But, there is no listing for a part that sounds like it would fit under the windshield bumpers and there is no part that attaches with 6 bolts through 6 holes.

Rule #2 is that IF IT IS NOT A PART OF WHAT YOU THINK IT IS, IT IS A PART OF SOME SEMI-LOGICAL ASSEMBLY. In the case of the 6 holes in the hood, they are positioned over the radiator so look under *Cooling.* That category is in Government Group 0501 on page 59 of the *TM-10-1186.* In this group I could find no part that was described as a part of the hood, but I quickly found under part number 51492 that 6 - ¼" 20 x½" screws are required for each MB to attach a *"top air* deflector to (the) hood".* Looking up 9 lines in the same category, there is a listing for Part A-2977, *Radiator top air deflector and seal assembly* (after truck serial number 108452) and that the number required is one per truck. The obvious (and correct) conclusion is that the six holes across the hood are for the bolts that hold this item in place.

I could cite many other examples, but this one shows clearly both the problem and the solution. As the radiator top air deflector is often missing on old jeeps, we depict one here for easy reference.

A-2295 is not a "hood stiffener" as many people suspect, but rather a part of the radiator. It is properly referred to as a Radiator Top Air Deflector and when it comes as an assembly it has a piece of horse-hair felt seal stapled to the bottom edge. When the hood is shut this thing deflects air through the radiator rather than allowing it to go over the top of the radiator. The screws that hold it to the hood are WO part number 51492. Yes, it does stiffen the hood.

A-2295

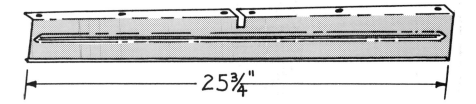

25¾"

A unique reversible train composed of jeeps at each end of 6 Japanese trailers hauled supplies in Burma. The line from Myitkyina to Mogaung had no provisions for turning the train around, so the push-me-pull-me technique shown here was adopted.

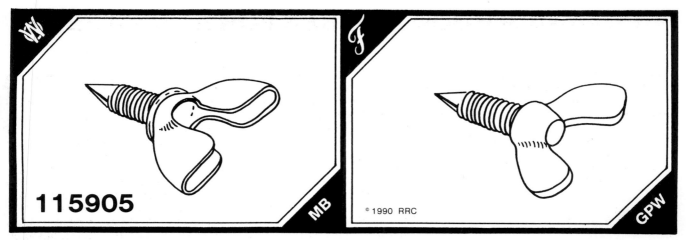

115905

The wing screws that hold the air filter to the firewall on WWII jeeps have an interesting difference - Willys typically used screws with stamped metal wings while those used by Ford usually had solid wings.

BLACKOUT (MAIN) LIGHT SWITCH (A-11867)

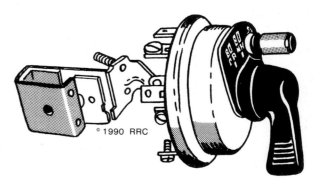

© 1990 RRC

(Probably used on MBs and GPWs from about 1 June 1944)

Late in the production of MBs and GPWs the blackout (main) light switch was changed from the original push-pull style to a rotary style switch installed in the same hole on the dash after adding a hole for the locking button.

Vehicles which came from the factory with the rotary switch *did not* have a black-

out *driving light* switch at the left end of the dash board, as that switch was incorporated in the rotary switch. Some vehicles in service were retrofitted with the rotary switch.

The rotary switch controls the entire lighting system of the MB or GPW it is on. It has a locking button at top center that functions in a similar way to the locking button on the push-pull switch. A thermal circuit breaker is a part of the rotary switch.

Some say the reason for the rotary switch was that it was less prone to being knocked out of adjustment by the left knee of the driver. I also suspect that the escutcheon plate on the rotary switch explaining which lights were being turned on by moving the lever eliminated a lot of confusion and nonconformity among drivers.

If you are going to put a rotary switch in a vehicle now equipped with a push-pull switch, here are the proper connections.

Terminal	Circuit	Cable Color or Circuit No.	
BAT	Ammeter	Red-white tracer	10
BHT	Blackout marker lights	Yellow-blue tracer	20
BHT	Blackout taillight	Yellow-blue tracer	24
BOD	Blackout driving light	Black-white tracer	19
BS	Blackout stoplight	White-black tracer	23
HT	Service taillight	Blue-white tracer	16
HT	Instrument light switch	Blue-white tracer	40
HT	Service headlight dimmer switch	Blue-white tracer	16
S	Service stoplight	Red-white tracer	22
SS	Trailer coupling socket	Red-black tracer	84
SS	Stoplight switch	Red-white tracer	75
SW	Stoplight switch	Green-black tracer	75
TT	Trailer coupling socket	Green-black tracer	83

Push switch shaft through instrument panel and place escutcheon plate over shaft. Secure in place with lockwasher and nut; install lever and tighten in place with screw. Attach ground cable to battery.

PICKING A HOOD NUMBER FOR A WWII JEEP

Hood numbers or USA registration numbers were assigned to each vehicle entering the service of the US armed forces during WWII. A block of numbers was assigned by the Government to each group of vehicles when the contract for production was let. It may be that some of these numbers were applied to the hood of the vehicle at the factory where it was produced, but it is certain that in most cases the number was applied when the Government took delivery.

I am frequently asked by owners of old vehicles how to determine what the correct hood number for a particular vehicle might have been. Reproduced below is a list of contracts for WWII ¼ tons and the hood numbers assigned to the contracts. You can quite easily determine the approximate position of any vehicle within a specific contract from the serial number of the vehicle itself (usually the number on the glove box door data plate which was taken from the frame vehicle identification number).

For example, Willys MB serial number 201878 was delivered on 1 November 1942 as that is the number and data on the glove box door data plate and the vehicle identification number on the frame. Willys MB serial numbering started at number 100001 so this particular jeep was *about* the 101878th one made (201878 minus 100001). To be where it is in the serial number range this jeep would have been *about* the 3376th jeep of 85,237 produced by Willys on US contract W-303-Ord.-2529. This contract was assigned hood numbers 20298626 to 20364862 so the 3376th vehicle *may* have had a hood number of *about* 203-02002.

These calculations presume that all vehicles ahead of the specific one in the contract got their numbers in proper sequence and were *not* shipped to a foreign government or a branch of service that did not use this hood numbering system (the US Marine Corps for example, used a five digit hood number such as 89552). That of course, is not true.

In any case, this is a reasonable method to determine an *approximate* hood number if you can't find the actual one in documentation or under the paint on the hood of a vehicle. It is also the method by which you can determine that the jeep at the front in the picture at the bottom of page 205 is likely to be a Willys. It has a hood number which was assigned to vehicles in the 8th Willys production contract and it was *probably* built on about Monday the 15th of March 1943. The serial number of this jeep would be *about* 233800, based on the hood number.

I have tried this mathematical process many times with known hood/serial numbers and found it to be plenty accurate for assigning a *probable* hood number to any jeep that needs one. As there never will be a method of calculating a *certain* hood number I'm happy to suggest you are far better off with a probable number than one that is completely out of sequence.

See also page 190

WILLYS-OVERLAND CONTRACTS

MODEL	YEAR	CONTRACT NUMBER	REGISTRATION NUMBER	QUANTITY
MA	1941	W-398-QM-8888	W2018932 - W2020431	1,500
MB	1942	W-398-QM-10757	W2031575 - W2047574	16,000
MB	1942	W-398-QM-10757	W2037614 - W2050213	2,600
MB	1942	DA-W-398-QM-189	2078697 - 2083803	16,608
MB	1942	W-398-QM-11423	2073506 - 2078606	
			2083804 - 2088730	
			20209017 - 20237883	43,601
MB	1942	W-398-QM-11423	20237844 - 20255483	17,600
MB	1942	W-398-QM-11423	20255484 - 20256076	593
MB	1942	W-303-ORD-2529	20298626 - 20364862	85,237
MB	1942	DA-W-398-QM-452	2092919 - 2092938	20

FORD MOTOR COMPANY CONTRACTS

MODEL	YEAR	CONTRACT NUMBER	REGISTRATION NUMBER	QUANTITY
GP	1941	W-398-QM-8887	2017422 - 2018921	1,500
GP	1941	W-398-QM-10262	2029494 - 2030493	1,000
GP	1941	DA-398-QM-27		1,150
GP	1941	W-398-QM-10651	234075 - 234124	50
GPW	1942	W-398-QM-10977	2054778 - 2069777	15,000
GPW	1942	W-398-QM-11424	20100000 - 20163145	63,146
GPW	1942	W-398-QM-13538	20185869 - 20209016	23,158
GPW	1942	W-374-ORD-2862	20364863 - 20443316	151,437
GPW	1944	W-20-018-ORD-4920		15,140

TWO INTERESTING FIELD MODIFICATIONS
EUROPEAN THEATRE OF OPERATIONS

Jeeps for transportation and fuel for stoves or to power other vehicles were in such great demand in Europe near the end and after the end of WWII that special precautions were taken to prevent the loss of either. The photos here depict two Field Modifications intended to prevent the loss of fuel and ¼ tons.

The upper photo shows a third Safety Strap Eye positioned on the dashboard of a jeep so the shift lever could be padlocked to it, thus immobilizing the jeep.

The lower photo depicts a slotted metal strap welded to the fuel tank cap and a matching one welded to the seat frame. A padlock through the slots in both straps prevented the removal of the fuel tank cap.

Both modifications were applied in France to the same slat grill MB. The vehicle was purchased surplus by a US Army of Occupation GI and returned to America in 1946. It was bought from the ex-GI by an MV collector in 1988.

MISCELLANEOUS INFORMATION

The section that follows contains an assortment of information pertaining to jeeps that has been reprinted from a wide variety of source material from the time of WWII. Some of it is from leading magazines of the day, some is from US Government publications and some is from instruction sheets that came with field modifications, accessories, or replacement parts kits for jeeps.

All the information included has two things in common: 1) it relates to jeeps, and 2) it is either difficult or expensive for an average enthusiast to acquire copies of the material in its original form.

One of the biggest problems I've faced in my quest for information about old GPWs and MBs is access. There are those who have accumulated large quantities of very obscure data regarding old jeeps, but most would never allow anyone to rummage through what they have. Still others "have" data but have it packed away in boxes that even *they* can't find.

Naturally, anything available in limited quantity that is sought after by many will go up in value. I have paid more for an old magazine containing a page or two of jeep information than the cost of this book. The sensible thing is to reprint the relevant data so that many may be able to evaluate it without the expense or difficulty of finding and buying a copy of the original magazines that contained the data.

I have also found that most people in the old jeep hobby are unfamiliar with the law regarding copyrights. They tend to think it would be illegal to reprint old manuals and other materials related to jeeps. While I am not a lawyer, the law that pertains to WWII era copyrights is simple enough that anyone can understand it. During the 1930s and 1940s any person or responsible agency that created an *ORIGINAL* written, musical or artistic work could, through the copyright process, gain an exclusive right to the use of his book, song or picture for a period of 28 years. At the end of that 28 year period the copyright owner could extend the copyright *once* for a period of another 28 years. Upon expiration of the copyright the material lapsed into the "public domain". That simply means it became everybody's property. Anyone may feel free to use it.

An understanding of the old copyright law (it was superseded by the Berne Convention Copyright Law in 1989) would make the curious ask, "How can the Imperial War Museum in London stamp "Copyright" on all the US Army Signal Corps photos they sell?" Good question - easy answer. They may stamp "Copyright" all over the photos but it is meaningless. Only the US Army Signal Corps or the Army photographer *could* have copyrighted the photos as *original* material. A party that comes into the possession of uncopyrighted or public domain material cannot copyright it. Originality is the key to copyrights.

My point is, of course, that if people understood the copyright process better more old and rare jeep data would be reproduced and made available for sale. That benefits everyone and hurts no one. If you are considering the reproduction of an old American manual or brochure which is marked "Copyright" you should consult a lawyer versed in such things or write the US Copyright Office in Washington DC. The Copyright Office will conduct a search of their records for a very reasonable fee.

Jeeps were such popular vehicles in post-war America that magazines like this one sponsored contests in which readers suggested modifications.

Jivin' up the
Jeep

THOUSANDS of Army jeeps are hitting the roads these days as car-hungry ex-GI's take advantage of their status as preferred buyers of surplus Government materials.

After the buyer has given all the neighborhood kids rides and has explained the front-wheel drive and the double reduction gear box to their inquisitive pappies, he begins to remember something he shouldn't have forgotten in the first place; that the jeep was designed specifically for military purposes, and that it has serious short-comings as either a family conveyance or as a commercial truck.

Very fortunately, it is easy to convert the jeep into an altogether respectable automobile. Here are a few ideas that have proved practical. MECHANIX ILLUSTRATED invites its readers to submit similar suggestions. Good snapshots are desirable; sketches or drawings are also acceptable. For material that can be published, MI will pay good rates promptly on acceptance. If enough contributions are received they will be made into a regular department.

Address: Joe Jeep, c/o MECHANIX ILLUSTRATED, 347 Madison Ave., New York 17, N. Y.

TOP BRACES: The top is the most poorly designed part of the jeep. The center bow doesn't support the canvas; the canvas supports it! To prevent undue wear on the material, brace the center bow with pieces of angle iron bolted to the frame.

SOFT SEATS: Some jeeps have solid bucket seats, others thin spring seats. In either case you'll find riding easier if you purchase a set of thick foam "rubber" kneeling pads of the same dimensions as the seats. These will help absorb the roughness that is characteristic of all jeep rides. For summer driving, cover the seats with washable cotton cases.

Small wonder jeeps have so many non-original holes in them when they finally fall into the hands of a collector.

Convert your Army jeep into a pleasure vehicle by adding a few gadgets the GI couldn't enjoy.

WINDSHIELD WIPER: Why the Army didn't equip jeeps with automatic windshield wipers seems to be a 64 dollar question. The intake manifold is already fitted for the air tube, so installing a Trico motor is easy. Extend tubing on outside as shown at right.

HOLD DOWN CLAMP: At idling speeds the hood rattles fiercely because it is clamped down only at the front end but not near the hinged end. A simple cure is to remove the useless hold-down clamps from the front end of the hood and mount as shown below.

IGNITION SWITCH: Most jeeps have a simple ignition switch, without locking means. If a regular car ignition lock is unobtainable, a padlock can be used. Mount an eyebolt in the dashboard against the switch and drill a hole for the lock yoke.

TAIL LIGHT: Save yourself a ticket by installing a 2 candle power lamp over the license plate before you drive at night. Connect the underground wire to one of the terminals intended for the trailer connections. Find the correct lead via trial and error.

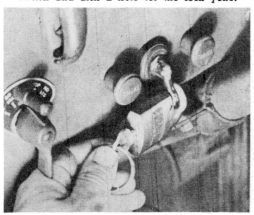

INSTRUCTIONS FOR UNCRATING AND ASSEMBLY OF VEHICLE

Uncrating Vehicle

Before the vehicle is packed in the crate, certain parts and assemblies are removed from the chassis and body in order to reduce the cubic contents as much as possible.

The parts or assemblies removed are securely strapped in place or packed in boxes fastened to the bottom of the crate.

To open the crate, remove nails from the metal band around top edge of crate.

Remove weather-proof paper and pull nails from metal bands over top on each end of the crate (fig. 2).

Pull spikes from side panel to the three joists on inside of top panel; also the nails from top cover panel to side and end panels.

The top cover can now be removed as one unit.

Packing Sheets

Remove the packing sheets and Instructions for Unpacking and Assembly Book from the envelope which is attached to the inside of the crate.

Remove the outside corner metal bands and the spikes through the corners of the crate (fig. 2), also the nails around the bottom of the side and end panels. Remove the side and end panels.

When all parts and assemblies have been removed from the individual packing boxes, and accessories from tool compartments located in the right and left rear corners of the body, check the parts according to the packing sheet list. Boxes are numbered 1, 2, 3, etc.

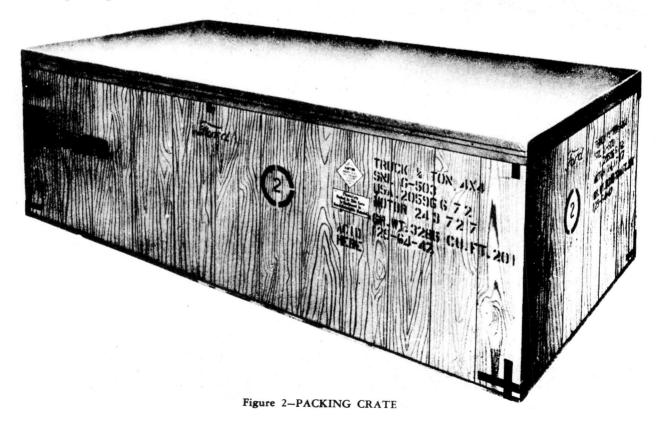

Figure 2—PACKING CRATE

Removal of Vehicle from Crate

Remove metal straps holding wheels in place, and remove the five wheels from inside of body.

Remove canvas top, side curtains from under passenger seat.

Remove chassis rear hold-down strap bolts and nuts (No. 1, fig. 3) from the rear cross joist on crate flooring, also the bolts and nuts from frame rear cross member.

Cut the metal band (No. 2, fig. 3) from around rear shock absorbers.

Raise rear end of vehicle about 2 feet which will release the strain on chassis front hold-down straps.

Remove the hold-down strap bolts and nuts (No. 1, fig. 4) from the front cross joist on the crate flooring and slide the straps off the front bumper.

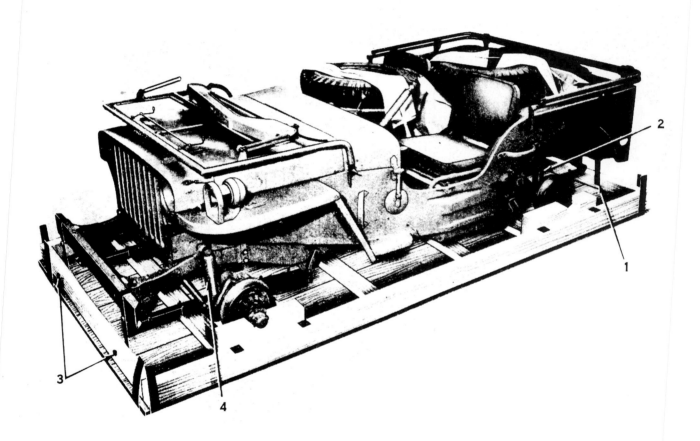

Figure 3—PACKING CRATE WITH TOP AND SIDES REMOVED (LEFT SIDE)

Cut the metal band (No. 2, fig. 4) from around front shock absorbers.

Install rear wheels (wheel nuts are in place on hub bolts). Left-hand threaded nuts (marked "L") are used on wheel hub bolts on left side of vehicle.

Remove battery acid container (No. 3, fig. 4).

Raise front of vehicle and install front wheels. (Wheel nuts are in place on hub bolts.)

Remove vehicle from crate.

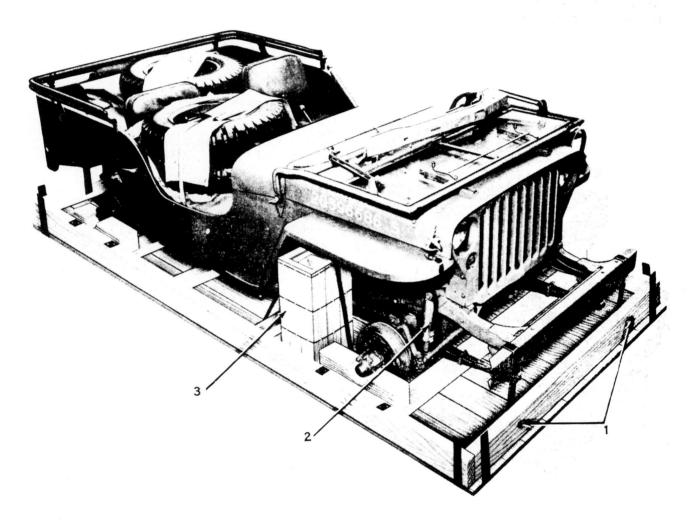

Figure 4—PACKING CRATE WITH TOP AND SIDES REMOVED (RIGHT SIDE)

Assembly

Install rear outside body handles, No. 1, fig. 5 (bolts and nuts are on handles).

Install spare wheel carrier to back of body, (No. 2, fig. 5) (bolts and nuts are in place on carrier).

Install rear bumperettes, No. 3, fig. 5 (attaching bolts and nuts are on bumperettes).

Install pintle hook on rear cross member, No. 4, fig. 5. The backing plate goes inside of frame (bolts and nuts are on pintle hook).

Install spare fuel container bracket (bolts are in bracket), No. 5, fig. 5.

Set front wheels in straight ahead position by placing a straight edge from rear wheel to front wheel so that it touches the tires at front and rear of each wheel.

Install steering wheel to steering post tube so that one spoke points downward toward driver's seat and is in line with steering post. No. 6, fig. 5.

Remove tape from horn opening, No. 1, fig. 6.

Remove block located under toe board which holds clutch depressed.

Remove tape from generator openings.

Remove tape from water pump.

Prepare Vehicle for Operation

Remove tape from the following units: air cleaner, No. 2, fig. 6; oil filler tube, No. 3, fig. 6; distributor, No. 4, fig. 6; engine ventilator tube, No. 5, fig. 6; battery filler caps, muffler tail pipe, radiator cap and radiator overflow pipe.

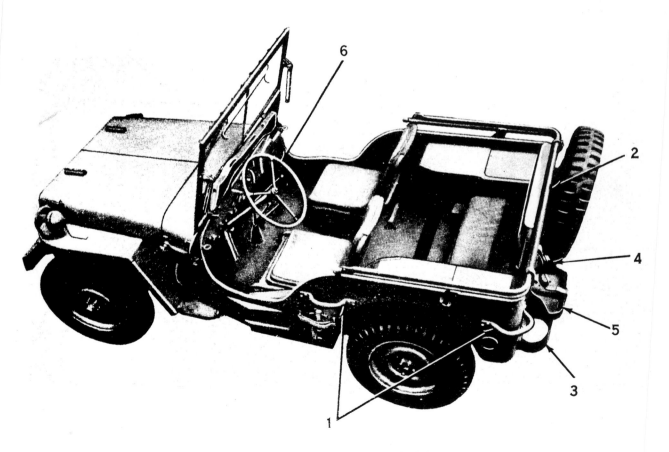

Figure 5—ASSEMBLY PROCEDURE

262

All bonds and bond connections must be clean.

Connect starter cable to large battery post and **ground** cable to small battery post.

Remove air cleaner, No. 6, fig. 6, by removing the two wing nuts, No. 7, fig. 6, loosen the two wing nuts on other side. Swing assembly toward radiator so as to clear studs and out toward right front fender, then slide assembly off studs.

To remove the air cleaner base from cover assembly use a wood block or a hammer handle inserted through top and tap sharply on base. Place one pint of engine oil of the specified grade in base, place cover assembly over base and press down, locking cover to base. Install assembly to brackets on dash.

Fill radiator, No. 8, fig. 6, with water, capacity 11 quarts. Use anti-freeze if necessary.

Fill engine with 4 quarts of engine oil through oil filler tube, No. 3, fig. 6.

Fill fuel tank through filler opening under driver's seat cushion. Replace cap, turning it to located position. Prime carburetor by operating the priming lever (located on rear side of the fuel pump body) up and down. This operates the fuel pump diaphragm manually and pumps the fuel from the fuel tank, filling the filter and carburetor bowl.

Turn rear view mirror up to position.

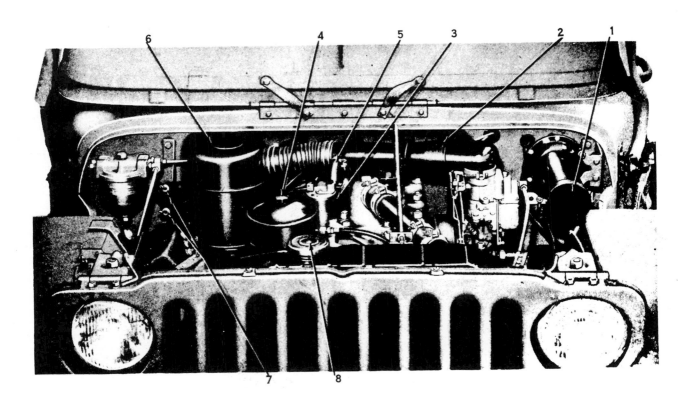

Figure 6—ENGINE COMPARTMENT

To Prepare Battery for Use

Dry-charged Storage Battery Type 17B-8811-2H (U. S. Army Specif.).

This battery is shipped with the plates in a partly charged condition. The vent plugs must be left tightly in place until ready to fill the battery.

The electrolyte to use for filling is dilute sulphuric acid. It must be pure and suitable for storage battery use and of proper specific gravity. (See table.) The temperature of the filling electrolyte should not exceed 90° Fahrenheit (32° Centigrade).

	Temperate Climate	Tropical* Climate
Filling Gravity	1.260	1.210
Maximum Temperature	110°F.	125°F.
Final Gravity	1.270-1.285	1.200-1.220

*A tropical climate is one in which water never freezes.

To Prepare Battery for Service

1. Unscrew vent plugs. Remove temporary paper discs from filling holes and discard them.

2. Fill each cell with the prepared electrolyte to ⅜ inch above top of separators.

3. Allow the battery to stand at least one hour after filling with electrolyte. If level has fallen, add electrolyte to restore it. Replace vent plugs in cells. If any electrolyte was spilled on battery, it should be removed by means of a cloth slightly dampened with a weak solution of baking soda and water.

4. A freshening charge at 8 amperes should be given before placing in service. Make certain the positive terminal of battery (marked POS or + or painted red) is connected to the positive of the charge circuit, and negative terminal of battery (marked NEG or — or painted black) is connected to negative of charge circuit.

5. Charge until four consecutive hourly readings show no rise in specific gravity for the lowest cell. If above rate is maintained, length of charging time will be at least 12 hours; lower rates will increase the time proportionately. If necessary to restore electrolyte level during charge, use only approved water.

6. After completion of charge, the gravity should be shown in table, corrected to 77° Fahrenheit and with the level ⅜ inch above top of separators. If it is not, adjust by removing some solution and replacing with approved water or electrolyte as required. Charge the battery to mix solution before testing again. NOTE: See battery manufacturer's special instructions on battery.

This vehicle should be serviced in accordance with instructions given in Technical Manual TM 9-803, paragraph 13, page 29, before being placed in operation.

This Motor Vehicle has been thoroughly tested and inspected before being packed for shipment. Like any other piece of machinery, to maintain it in proper operating condition, it should be lubricated and receive periodic systematic inspection as outlined in TM 9-803 Technical Manual which is furnished with each vehicle.

The following pages outline how to remove the vehicle from the packing case and the sequence of operations necessary in the assembly.

FORD MOTOR COMPANY
Dearborn, Mich., U. S. A.

NEW TYPE RETURNABLE CRATE
INSTRUCTIONS FOR UNCRATING & ASSEMBLY OF VEHICLE
¼ TON 4 x 4

Before the vehicle is placed in the Wooden Returnable Crate, it has received preservative treatment to prevent corrosion. Certain parts and assemblies have been removed in order to reduce the crate cubic content. These parts or assemblies are securely strapped in the body.

TO DISMANTLE THE CRATE

Remove the 16 - ⅜'' x 4'' machine bolts around the sides and ends of top panel, Ordnance Part No. 7068965.

Remove top panel from crate.

Remove the 24 - ⅜'' x 2'' carriage bolts from upper and lower metal corner brackets.

Remove 16 - ⅜'' x 4'' machine bolts around the sides and ends of the bottom panel. Ordnance Part No. 7068962.

Remove side panels, Part No. 7068963 and end panels, Part No. 7068964 from bottom panel.

REMOVAL OF VEHICLE FROM CRATE BOTTOM

Cut metal strap holding wheel and tire to radiator guard. (Remove wheel and tire.)

Remove rear lower Chassis hold-down strap bolts and nuts from the cross joist on crate bottom panel, Ordnance Part No. 7068962, and the bolts and nuts from frame rear cross member.

Remove front chassis hold-down strap bolts and nuts from the cross joist on bottom panel and slide metal straps off the bumper.

Remove electrolyte Carboy from under left front fender.

Cut and remove metal straps holding wheels and box of parts in body.

ASSEMBLY

Raise rear end of vehicle and install rear wheels. (Hub bolt nuts in place on hub bolts.) Left hand thread nuts have groove around hexagon head and are used on wheel hub bolts on left side of vehicle.

Raise front end of vehicle and install front wheels. Roll vehicle off of crate bottom panel.

Remove sealing tape from end of steering column. (Steering wheel nut, horn button, keys and body drain plugs are in a bag in the glove compartment.)

Set front wheels in straight ahead position by placing straight edge from rear wheel to front wheel so that it touches the tires front and rear.

Install steering wheel on steering post tube so that one spoke points toward driver's seat and is in line with steering post.

ASSEMBLY — (Cont'd.)

Install front and rear body outside handles. (Bolts and nuts in handle.)

Install spare wheel carrier and support to back of body. (Bolts and nuts in place.)

Install Pintle hook on rear cross member. The reinforcing backing plate goes inside frame. (Safety chain eye bolts go in lower holes with offset down.)

Install spare gasoline can bracket assembly to left of spare wheel carrier. (Attaching bolts and nuts in bracket.)

Install rear Bumperettes. (Attaching bolts and nuts in bumperettes.)

Install Top Bow assembly by placing ends through top bow pivots on rear brackets and then insert bow ends in front brackets.

Install the two ¼" drain plugs in body floor front compartment.

Install gun scabbard. (Attaching bolts in scabbard.)

IMPORTANT

Remove sealing tape and plugs from following units: generator, distributor, glove compartment and tool box locks and muffler tail pipe. Remove paint from reflectors, blackout and tail lamp lenses with gasoline or cleaning solvent. Remove paper from front of radiator and wood block between clutch pedal and dash.

CONDITIONING OF VEHICLE

Check lubricant in transmission, transfer case, engine, front and rear axles. Remove air cleaner oil base by releasing the two spring snap fasteners. See that there is one pint of oil in base in accordance with Technical or Maintenance Manual. Reinstall base to cleaner.

Check Coolant in Radiator.

Inflate tires to 35 lbs. pressure.

Fill fuel tank through filler opening under driver's seat cushion. Replace cap, turning to lock position. Prime carbureter by operating the priming lever up and down located on rear side of fuel pump body. (Leave lever in down position when system is full.) This operates the fuel pump diaphragm assembly and pumps the fuel from the fuel tank; filling the filter and carbureter bowls.

To prepare the battery, remove sealing discs, located on top or under vent plugs, make certain that vent holes in all plugs are open. Connect Battery Cables to Battery Terminals.

Fill each cell to ⅜" above the plates with electrolyte (acid and water) in carboy removed from under left front fender.

Let battery stand one hour, if liquid levels have fallen, add electrolyte to restore level. Screw vent plugs in place. See instructions on tag attached to battery.

NOTE: This vehicle should be serviced in accordance with instructions given in Technical or Maintenance Manual.

Date: February, 1945.   PART NO. A-17462
    Willys-Overland Motors, Inc.
    Toledo, Ohio U.S.A.

TRAILER ELECTRICAL CONNECTION
and
SAFETY CHAIN KIT

Part No. A-6544
(Marine Part No. A-6593)

Willys Model MB ¼-Ton 4 x 4 Truck
Ford Model GPW ¼-Ton 4 x 4 Truck

This kit consists of a coupling socket for electrical connections to the trailer with a cover to install inside the tool compartment to protect the socket. Eye bolts are also supplied for the attachment of the trailer safety chains. All the necessary fittings and attaching parts are included in the kit.

The following tools are required to install these parts:

1—$\frac{7}{16}$" end wrench
1—$\frac{3}{8}$" end wrench
1—$\frac{7}{8}$" thin wall socket
1—6" socket extension
1—socket handle
1—10" screw driver
1—4" screw driver
1—electric drill
1—$\frac{17}{32}$" drill
1—$\frac{9}{32}$" drill
1—$\frac{7}{8}$" drill
1—center punch
1—mechanics hammer
1—6" metal measuring scale
1—metal compass
1—12" half round file

A template is supplied as a part of these instructions, to correctly locate the socket and reflector.

First install the safety chain eye bolts Part No. A-6393 (Marine A-6744). Remove the two lower bolts holding the pintle hook to the rear of the frame and drill these holes $\frac{17}{32}$". Install the eye bolts with the offset down and tighten securely using lockwashers Part No. 5009 and nuts Part No. 6163.

Remove all equipment from the left tool compartment and remove the left rear reflector. Discard the screws and nuts as the screws were swaged in assembly and new ones are supplied in the kit.

Next cut the template as indicated and place it against the back of the body with the cut out section against the tail light and the lower cut edge flush with the lower edge of the body panel.

Make sure the template is correctly located and center punch for the seven holes required. Drill the six holes used to mount the socket and reflector $\frac{9}{32}$". Cut the hole for the electric socket $2\frac{7}{8}$" in diameter.

On the floor of the left tool compartment draw a line $3\frac{7}{16}$" forward from the inside of the body rear panel (Fig. 2). Also draw a line $3\frac{3}{16}$" to the left from the inside tool compartment partition. At the intersection of these two lines, center punch and drill a $\frac{7}{8}$" hole and install grommet Part No. 345961.

Reinstall the reflector at the new holes using two screws Part No. 52834, two lockwashers Part No. 52707 and two nuts Part No. 52847. Place the nuts and lockwashers on the inside of the tool compartment. (Should it be desired to balance up the rear of the body by relocating the right reflector, reverse the template and center punch for the reflector holes only. Extra screws and nuts are included in the kit.)

Next remove the metal cover which protects the terminals at the rear end of the socket Part No. A-6019. Connect the wiring harness Part No. A-6355 (end with same length wires) to the terminals which are exposed as follows:—

Green wire with two black tracers to terminal marked "TL" (Tail Light).

Red wire with two black tracers to terminal marked "SL" (Stop Light).

The small terminal of the black ground wire with two white tracers Part No. A-6356 should be attached to the terminal marked "GR" (Ground).

Be sure all connections are tight and replace the cover.

The electric coupling socket is supplied in the kit partially disassembled. The attaching parts with the exception of four internal and external lockwashers Part No. 53024 are placed in a cloth bag. Mount the socket on the body panel in the following manner.

Put the two longer screws—$\frac{1}{4}$"-28 thd. x 1" through the holes in the cover hinge. Place the dust shield retainer ring over the screws followed by the rubber dust shield with the slot in the center opening away from the cover hinge. Place the two screws through the two upper mounting holes and place internal and external lockwashers Part No. 53024 over each screw followed by the socket body with drain hole down. Install lockwashers Part No. 52707 and nuts Part No. 52847 loosely. It is important that the internal and external lockwashers be installed to secure a good ground connection. Install the two lower screws $\frac{1}{4}$"-28 thd. x $\frac{3}{4}$" with the lockwashers in correct position. Place the ground wire terminal over the lower inside screw and tighten all four nuts to hold the socket firmly in position.

Thread the wiring harness through the grommet and fasten it in position beside the vehicle wiring harness using the new clips supplied. Place the new clips in the same position as those originally used to fasten the vehicle wiring harness using the original screws. The positions at which the harness is clipped in place are given below:

Clip Part No. A-5449 at floor rear reinforcement

Clip Part No. A-1289 at the rear foot rest

Clip Part No. A-5450 with loom Part No. A-5090 at the fuel tank sump

Clip Part No. A-5449 at rear floor pan reinforcement

Clip Part No. A-5449 at the frame cross member

In addition to the above clips, tape the trailer harness to the vehicle harness at the frame cross member in front of the fuel tank sump, also use new screw Part No. 50604 and clip Part No. A-5449 in the two positions under the toe-board.

Bring the harness up on the forward side of the dash, then through the dash with the vehicle wiring harness and connect the terminals to the main light switch as given below:—

Connect the green wire with 2 black tracers to the switch terminal marked "TT" (Trailer Tail).

Connect the red wire with 2 black tracers to the terminal marked "SS" (Stop Light Switch).

If a trailer is available place the electric plug in the socket and test the lights. Operation of the main light switch will control the service tail lights on the trailer and operation of the stop light switch will control the trailer service stop lights, providing the trailer switch is turned to the service position (to the left). Test the blackout system by operating the blackout lights on the truck with the trailer switch turned to the blackout position (to the right).

After testing the lights, install trailer electric plug housing cover, Part No. A-4592, designed to protect the socket inside the tool compartment.

As shown by the illustration (Fig. 3) draw a line $5\frac{3}{32}$" down from the top edge of the rear body panel. Draw a line $3\frac{15}{32}$" to the right from the left rear panel joint. Where these two lines cross, center punch and drill $\frac{9}{32}$". The lower socket cover holding screw hole must be drilled from underneath the wheel housing. As shown in the illustration, (Fig. 1) draw a line $1\frac{3}{4}$" upward from the edge of the angle in the tool compartment floor, also draw a line $4\frac{15}{16}$" toward the wheel housing flange from the inside of the body. Where these lines cross, center punch and drill $\frac{9}{32}$". Place the cover in position using screws Part No. 52168, plain washer Part No. 50937, lockwasher Part No. 53084 and hexagon nut Part No. 52217.

At the rear panel the screw head should be placed on the outside and the plain washer inside bearing against the cover. At the tool compartment floor the screw head should be placed inside the tool compartment with a plain washer next to the cover and the third plain washer next to the floor underneath the tool compartment completing the installation.

WILLYS-OVERLAND MOTORS, INC.
Toledo, Ohio

Instruction Sheet Form No. A-6358   Date 2-8-44

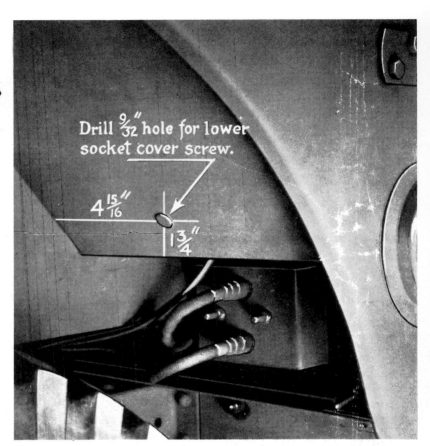

Drill $\frac{9}{32}$" hole for lower socket cover screw.

$4\frac{15}{16}$"

$1\frac{3}{4}$"

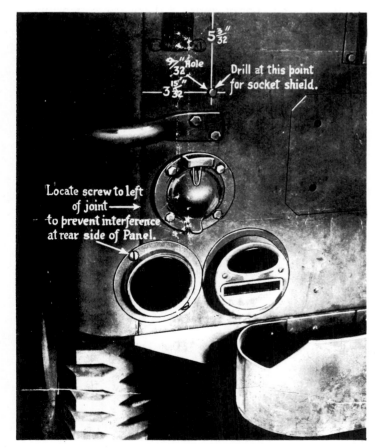

$5\frac{3}{32}$"

$\frac{9}{32}$" hole

Drill at this point for socket shield.

$3\frac{15}{32}$"

Locate screw to left of joint → to prevent interference at rear side of Panel.

Tool compartment inside Partition

2

Left tool Compartment floor.

Drill $\frac{7}{8}$" hole where lines intersect

$3\frac{3}{16}$"

$3\frac{7}{16}$"

Rear Body Panel

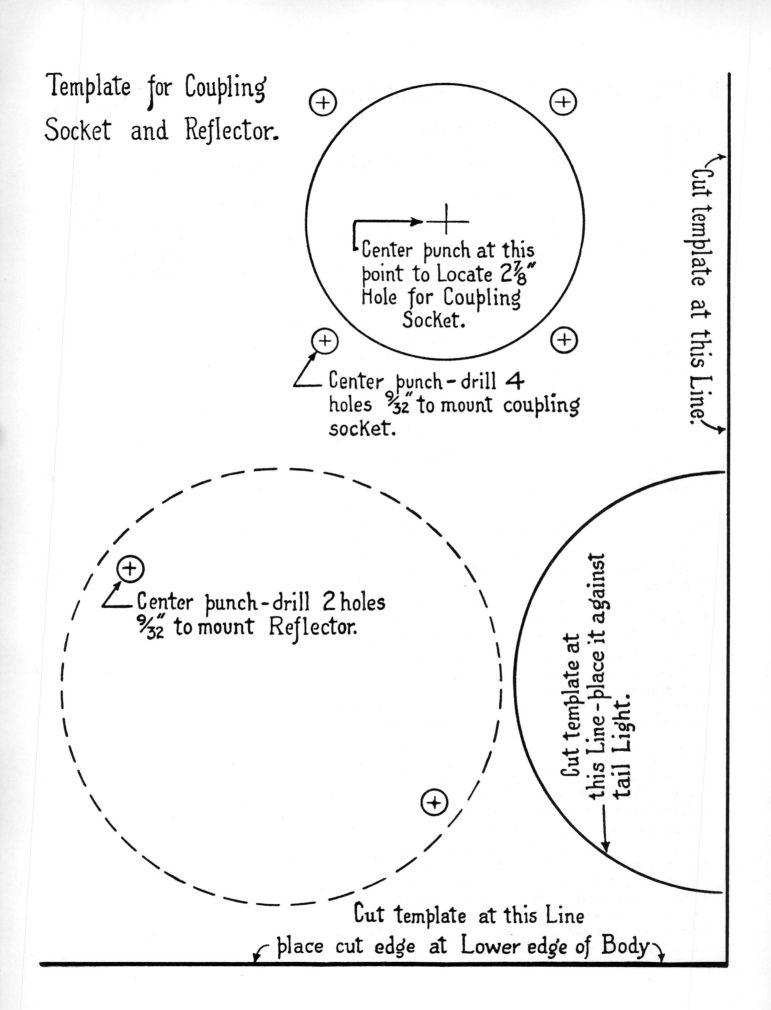

Template for Coupling Socket and Reflector.

Center punch at this point to Locate 2⅞" Hole for Coupling Socket.

Center punch-drill 4 holes ⁹⁄₃₂" to mount coupling socket.

Center punch-drill 2 holes ⁹⁄₃₂" to mount Reflector.

Cut template at this Line.

Cut template at this Line - place it against tail Light.

Cut template at this Line place cut edge at Lower edge of Body

INSTRUCTIONS FOR INSTALLING
TRICO *Vacuum* WINDSHIELD WIPERS
on "JEEPS"

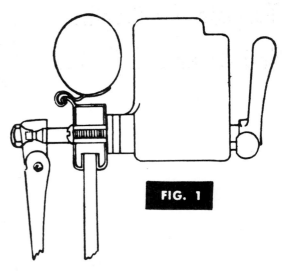

FIG. 1

1. Enlarge present windshield wiper hole in frame to 13/32" diameter. Move L.H. hood windshield rest block 2" to left in order to clear wiper arm when shield is down.

2. Install vacuum wiper motor as shown (Sketch in Fig. 1). Drill 7/32" diameter holes 1-13/16" each way from center line of shaft hole, or position wiper motor in present shaft hole and scribe these hole locations. Attach motor securely with screws and lock washers provided.

3. Form the long metal tubing to match the windshield frame as illustrated by Fig. 2 and fasten by means of clips and self-tapping screws supplied. Drill .166 diameter holes, No. 19 drill.

4. Remove intake manifold if drilling and tapping is necessary. Drill and tap intake manifold with a 1/8 inch pipe tap (use 21/64 inch drill). NOTE: If car is equipped with outlet plug, no drilling is necessary - simply remove plug and attach reducing bushing supplied with wiper set as illustrated in Fig. 3. Fasten short metal tube to intake manifold using compression nut and body supplied. Be sure to tighten firmly in place.

5. Connect the short tube to the long tube attached to the windshield frame by means of the short rubber hose supplied. Make sure that the hose is looped properly to permit folding down of the windshield (Fig. 4).

6. Connect upper end of vacuum line to windshield motor using other short length of rubber hose supplied. NOTE: When two wipers are installed, use the fitting to carry hose to right hand wiper (Fig. 5).

7. Start motor, turn wiper motor on, then off, to bring piston in parked position. Place wiper arm on end of shaft in parked position (as shown) and tighten securely with arm nut. NOTE: Hold arm firmly while tightening nut so as to prevent any unnecessary strain on the wiper mechanism. Hook blade on to arm to complete installation.

FIG. 2

FIG. 3

FIG. 4

FIG. 5

Editor's note: notice by-the-book placement of hood star in Figure 4 above.

Manufactured by

Trico Products Corporation   Buffalo, New York

WORLD'S LARGEST MANUFACTURER OF WINDSHIELD EQUIPMENT

5804

PRINTED IN U.S.A.

INSTALLATION INSTRUCTIONS

CONNECTOR - - Windshield Wiper - Hand - - FOR DUAL INSTALLATION
ORDNANCE STOCK NUMBER G503-5,700,003

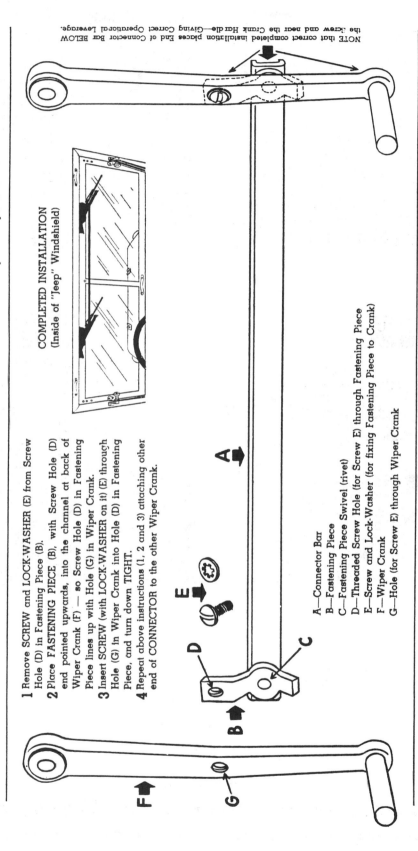

NOTE that correct completed installation places End of Connector Bar BELOW the Screw and near the Crank Handle—Giving Correct Operational Leverage.

COMPLETED INSTALLATION
(Inside of "Jeep" Windshield)

1 Remove SCREW and LOCK-WASHER (E) from Screw Hole (D) in Fastening Piece (B).

2 Place FASTENING PIECE (B), with Screw Hole (D) end pointed upwards, into the channel at back of Wiper Crank (F) — so Screw Hole (D) in Fastening Piece lines up with Hole (G) in Wiper Crank.

3 Insert SCREW (with LOCK-WASHER on it) (E) through Hole (G) In Wiper Crank into Hole (D) in Fastening Piece, and turn down TIGHT.

4 Repeat above instructions (1, 2 and 3) attaching other end of CONNECTOR to the other Wiper Crank.

A—Connector Bar
B—Fastening Piece
C—Fastening Piece Swivel (rivet)
D—Threaded Screw Hole (for Screw E) through Fastening Piece
E—Screw and Lock-Washer (for fixing Fastening Piece to Crank)
F—Wiper Crank
G—Hole (for Screw E) through Wiper Crank

Used on Army "Jeeps" - to connect for dual wiping Two "WINDSHIELD WIPER ASSEMBLIES - HAND - SINGLE . . . ORDNANCE STOCK NO. G503-5,700,002" - - this "CONNECTOR" makes the movement of ONE Wiper operate BOTH Wipers . . . thus, a rider cleans driver's side of windshield—while cleaning his own.

CONNECTOR - - Windshield Wiper - Hand - - FOR DUAL INSTALLATION
ORDNANCE STOCK NUMBER G503-5,700,003

Used on Army "Jeeps" to connect Two "WINDSHIELD WIPER ASSEMBLIES - HAND - SINGLE . . . ORDNANCE STOCK NO. G503-5,700.003" - . this "CONNECTOR" makes the movement of ONE Wiper operate BOTH Wipers . . . thus, a rider cleans driver's side of windshield — while cleaning his own.

This "CONNECTOR" can be used only to connect two individual wiper units — Ordnance Stock Number G503-5,700,003.

This "CONNECTOR" comes in one assembled piece
— as shown below — consisting of parts indicated:

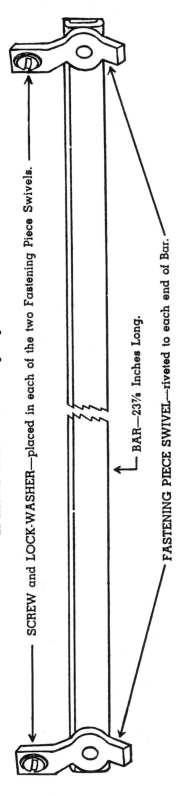

SCREW and LOCK-WASHER—placed in each of the two Fastening Piece Swivels.

BAR—23⅜ Inches Long.

FASTENING PIECE SWIVEL—riveted to each end of Bar.

INSTALL AS SHOWN ON OTHER SIDE OF THIS SHEET

Manufactured in U. S. A. by

THE ANDERSON COMPANY — GARY. INDIANA

Printed in U. S. A.

ANCO Form No. 04-0108

INSTRUCTIONS FOR UNPACKING AND ASSEMBLY OF ¼-TON TRAILER MB-T

The unpacking and assembly instructions are in a waterproof envelope with the packing slips which list all assemblies also attaching parts packed in cartons No. 1 and 2. It is tacked in the upper Left Hand Corner of the Case.

The only difference between the Army Quartermaster Corps (QMC) parts and those used on the Marine (NOM) jobs is the color of the paint.

The part numbers used in the text are QMC, therefore when a NOM job is to be assembled, refer to Fig. 6 index for identification of parts.

Unpacking—

Remove metal strap around top edge of the case, which holds the waterproof paper and remove the paper.

Remove metal straps across the top of case and pull out nails around outer edge of the top panel.

Pull the spikes through the top frame in the Ends of the 2″ x 8″ and 2″ x 4″ Cross Joints, Fig. 1, No. 1, on each side, which supports the upper Body, No. 2. Remove top panel from case.

Remove the metal corner straps Fig. 1, No. 5 at top and bottom, remove spikes through each corner of Case at Top and Bottom. Remove nails and spikes around outer edge of side and end panels at case flooring. Remove side and end panels allowing upper body to rest on lower body. Then remove body with the 2″ x 8″ Cross Joists attached. Remove the eight carriage bolts No. 4 which hold joists to body.

Cut metal straps, Fig. 2, No. 1 and remove cartons No. 2.

Cut metal straps Fig. 3, No. 1 and remove Lunette Eye and bracket assemblies No. 2, axle assemblies No. 3, and "A" frame channels and Brake Cables No. 4.

Cut metal straps Fig. 4, No. 1, holding Tires and Wheels. Remove wood blocking, No. 2, Tarpaulins, No. 3, Wheels and Tires, No. 4, Support Legs, No. 5, and Springs, No. 6.

In the first trailers shipped the Brake Cable and Conduit Assemblies were strapped to wood sills. Later these assemblies were placed inside of "A" frame channel and wired in place.

Cut metal straps Fig. 5, No. 1 holding fenders, No. 2, remove fenders and wood frame from lower body Fig. 3, No. 5.

Remove the spikes and nails from metal straps and driven into ends of 2″ x 8″ cross joists Fig. 3, No. 6. Remove body from case flooring with 2″ x 8″ cross joists attached. Remove the eight carriage bolts holding joists to body.

Lay out the assemblies and attaching parts from cartons so that they can be readily identified and remove sealing tape from Brake Drums.

When making the assembly refer to Fig. 6 and also to pictures in the Maintenance Manual.

Assembly—

To start assembly, turn the trailer body bottom side up. (CAUTION: The left side is the right side when the body is bottom side up; chalk mark bottom of body. In the following text left or right refers to the trailer on its wheels). Next attach the Spring Shackle Bracket, Part No. A-6449 on the left side member and rear intermediate cross member with the flat side of the brace towards the front, and Part No. A-6455 on the right hand side. Eight hexagon head screws, 3/8"-24 x 1", Part No. 50847, with Nut, No. 50922 and Palnut No. 52909 are used to attach these brackets, inserting the screws with the heads toward the body. Tighten the palnuts only sufficiently to act as locking nuts.

Next install the Spring Pivot Bracket, No. A-6447, on the left side member and front intermediate cross member with the flat side of the brace toward the front, then install Part No. A-6467 on the right hand side. Use same size screws and nuts as were used for spring rear bracket installation.

Raise both shock absorbers to a perpendicular position and place Axle Assembly Part No. A-1891 across body between spring brackets with wheel studs marked with "L" on end of studs, to the left side.

Next, install the Springs, Part No. A-612. Both springs are the same and the bushed end goes toward the front. Install the front Spring Pivot Bolts, No. A-6776 in the front spring brackets from the outside with the grease hole toward the body. Tap bolts in until the serrated part enters the bracket, then start Nut No. 53043, tapping on head of bolt and tightening nut until the head of bolt rests against the bracket; back off nut 1/6 turn and insert cotter pin Part No. 5021, also install grease fitting Part No 392909 in head of bolt.

Spring Shackle U-Bolt and Bushing assembly No. A-1893 LH consists of U-Bolt No. A-513, Bushing No. 635532 (Notched Head) and No. 634432 Bushing RH Thread.

Spring Shackle U-Bolt and Bushing assembly No. A-1894 consists of U-Bolt No. A-514 and 2 bushings No. 634432. Before assembly remove tape from around bushings.

Next, install Spring Shackles Part No. A-513 LH and No. A-514 RH from inside, see Fig. 16-17-18 in Maintenance Manual. First put Grease Seal Retainer, Part No. A-1252 on shackle with open end towards threads, then install Seal No. A-515, after which put shackle in place; Shackle Part No. A-513 with left hand thread goes on right side with the left hand threaded end in the spring eye. It is identified by a small lug on the shank of the shackle. Start left hand threaded Spring Shackle Bushing No. 635532 (with Notched head) on right rear shackle at spring end; insert the other bushing Part No. 634432 and tighten equally. (Left Shackle and Bushings are right hand thread). Upper bushings tighten against the bracket and lower bushings should have 1/32" clearance between head and spring eye.

Raise axle so that the spring seat is against spring with center bolt head in hole of spring seat. Install spring to Axle Clips No. A-6511, then Spring Clip Plates No. A-571 and A-572 with shock absorbers attached using Lockwashers No. 53044 and Nuts No. A-6508. Tighten securely. (See Fig. 16, Maintenance Manual).

Slip Brake Cable and Conduit Assembly Part No. A-6406 through conduit bracket on brake backing plate, (See Fig. 8, Page 13 Maintenance Manual). Have spring and washer to the rear of the bracket. Insert Screw No. 6609 in bracket and tighten in place with Lockwasher No. 51833 and Nut No. 5910 after placing end of conduit flush with bracket. Attach cable end to brake cam lever at backing plate, using Clevis Pin No. A-6526 and Cotter Pin No. 5067. Slip other end of brake conduit into Clamp No. A-6766 and attach to front intermediate frame cross member with Screws No. 53048, Lockwashers No. 53047 and Nut No. 50802. Make the same installation on the opposite side.

On Cable Hook Bolt No. A-6516 put Nut No. 50802. Hook this bolt in short arm of bell crank with open end away from body, then put brake cable through Equalizer, Part No. A-6768 so open side will be away from the body, stretch cables several times and install equalizer on hook bolt after which put on Nut No. 50802 then a Palnut No. 53049.

When assembling the draw bar which consists of the "A" frame channels, lunette eye and draw bar bracket and "A" frame channel clamps install all bolts, lockwashers and nuts finger tight until after complete assembly, then tighten the four "A" frame channel clamp bolt nuts first and follow with other bolt nuts, lock those nuts with cotter pins where specified.

First insert the ends of the "A" Frame Channels, Part No. A-6381, in the gussets at front intermediate cross member with Screws No. 53036, Lockwashers No. 53045 and Nuts No. 50811. Next, install left and right Frame Clamps Nos. A-6027 (Left) and A-6028 (Right) over "A" frame channels and attach to front cross member with Screws No. 53038, Lockwashers No. 52046 and Nut No. 50922.

Install Lunette Eye and Draw Bar Bracket Assembly Part No. A-1890 to "A" Frame Channels Part No. A-6381 with four Hex. Head Screws $\frac{7}{16}$"-20 x 1" Part No. 6518, Nut No. 53041 and Cotter Pin No. 5021. Install Safety Chains Part No. A-6392 over Screw No. A-6515 then through front hole, then the other chain, and lock with Nut Part No. 53039 and Cotter Pin No. 5108. Open side of hooks must be toward Lunette Eye. Install Support Bracket No. A-6371 with Screw No. A-6519 ($\frac{3}{4}$"-16 x $3\frac{3}{8}$") Nut No. 53039 and Cotter Pin No. 5108. Next attach Support Leg, Part No. A-6368 with foot towards the rear, using Screws No. A-6527, Nuts No. 53040 and Cotter Pins No. 5137.

Remove the Blackout Light Switch Fig. 6, No. 27 located at the right front corner of the body. Remove the cover and gasket held in place with three screws. Attach the coupling Socket Cable No. A-6387 as follows:

First remove the rubber insulating tips from both the brown and white wires. Thread the brown wire through the rubber grommet in the switch body which lines up with the switch terminal marked "T." Reinstall the rubber insulating tip and connect securely to terminal "T". Thread the white wire through the other rubber grommet in the switch body—reinstall the rubber insulating tip and connect to the switch terminal marked "S". The cover should then be replaced with the gasket in position and the switch assembly remounted with the rubber grommets away from the body.

Attach red wire to right front gusset plate for "Ground" putting Screw No. 5113 through $\frac{7}{32}$" hole from front side then put on Lockwasher No. 53023 (to secure a good ground) then wire terminal, Lockwasher No. 52221 and Nut No. 6352. Tighten securely. Bring cable across on top of right frame channel and attach with Clip No. A-6809 and with Metal Screw No. 52993, with clip towards the rear. Bring cable on inside of the frame and attach to inside of frame with Clip No. A-6809, Screw No. 5113, Lockwasher No. 52221 and Nut No. 6352. Thread wire over draw bar bracket and up to attach on top of bracket with Clip No. A-6335, Washer No. 52706 and Screw No. 51738.

Install wheels. Note the Left Hand Threaded Nuts No. A-475 with notches around the Hexagon sides are used on Left Hand Wheel Hub studs with letter "L" on end.

Turn vehicle over sideways onto wheels, and install fenders, Part No. A-4179 using Screws No. 53031 and Plain Washers No. 53032 on outside of fender. Place on underside a Plain Washer No. 53032, Lockwasher No. 52046 and Nut No. 53033.

Attach Hand Brake Rod Part No. A-6400 to Hand Brake Lever, Part No. A-6378 and Use Cotter Pin No. 5020.

Attach Hand Brake Lever No. A-6378 to front cross member on right side so that it pulls to the right side, using Screws No. 53050, Lockwasher No. 53047 and Nuts No. 50802.

Install Hand Brake Rod in bell crank and lock with Flat Washer No. 53051 and Cotter Pin No. 5020.

Next adjust hand brake cable. Pull up the hand brake lever two notches, raise both wheels off floor; take up on bolt adjustment at equalizer until brakes drag slightly when wheels are turned by hand, then lock adjustment. When hand brake is released, wheels must turn without brake drag. Next plug connector in socket on truck and check for operation of lights.

Two spare Safety Chain Eye Bolts No. A-6393, Nuts No. 6163 and Lockwashers No. 5009 are furnished with the trailer parts in case the truck is not so equipped. To install, remove the two lower pintle hook bolts. Drill frame holes out to $\frac{17}{32}$". Install eye bolts with the eye offset down and tighten securely.

ILLUSTRATIONS

I

QMC	NOM	
1.		Cross Joist 2″ x 8″
2. A-3978	A-4178	Body Assembly
3.		Cleat 1¾″ x 48″
4.		Carriage Bolts
5.		Metal Corner Strap

II

1.		Metal Strap
2.		Carton Boxes

III

1.		Metal Strap
2. A-1890	A-6682	Lunette Eye & Draw Bar Bracket
3. A-1891	A-1899	Axle Assembly
4. A-6381	A-6689	"A" Frame Channel
5. A-3978	A-4178	Body Assembly

IV

1.		Metal Strap
2.		Wood Blocking
3. A-4048	A-4177	Tarpaulin Assembly
4. A-5597	A-5739	Wheel and Tire Assembly
5. A-6368	A-6765	Support Leg
6. A-612	A-6764	Spring

V

1.		Metal Strap
2. A-4179	A-4180	Fender

VI

1. A-6368	A-6765	Support Leg
2. A-6371	A-6773	Support Bracket
3. A-6381	A-6689	"A" Frame Channel
4. A-6027	A-6690	"A" Frame Channel Clamp Left
5. A-6516	A-6516	Hand Brake Cable Hook Bolt

QMC	NOM	
6. A-6768	A-6769	Hand Brake Cable Equalizer
7. A-6447	A-6684	Spring Pivot Bracket—Front Left
8. A-5597	A-5739	Wheel and Tire Assembly
9. A-6766	A-6767	Brake Conduit Clamp
10. A-6406	A-6406	Hand Brake Cable and Conduit Assembly
11. A-571	A-6770	Spring Clip Plate and Shaft Assembly—Left
12. A-169	A-169	Shock Absorber
13. A-612	A-6764	Spring
14. A-6449	A-6686	Spring Shackle Bracket—Rear Left
15. A-514	A-514	Spring Shackle "U" Bolt—Right
16. A-1891	A-1889	Axle Assembly
17. A-572	A-6771	Spring Clip Plate and Shaft Assembly—Right
18. A-612	A-6764	Spring
19. A-513	A-513	Spring Shackle U Bolt—Left
20. 634432	634432	Shackle Bushing
21. A-4109	A-4109	Body Drain
22. A-6455	A-6687	Spring Shackle Bracket — Rear Right
23. 635532	635532	Shackle Bushing
24. A-4179	A-4180	Fender
25. A-6467	A-6685	Spring Pivot Bracket—Front Right
26. A-3978	A-4178	Body Assembly
27. A-6021	A-6021	Blackout Switch
28. A-6378	A-6683	Hand Brake Lever Assembly
29. A-6028	A-6691	"A" Frame Channel Clamp—Right
30. A-6400	A-6775	Hand Brake Rod
31. A-6387	A-6387	Coupling Socket Cable Assembly
32. A-6392	A-6688	Trailer Safety Shain Assembly
*33. A-1890	A-6682	Lunette Eye and Draw Bar Bracket

* Note A-6541—A-6681—No. 2 and 33 Assembled together.

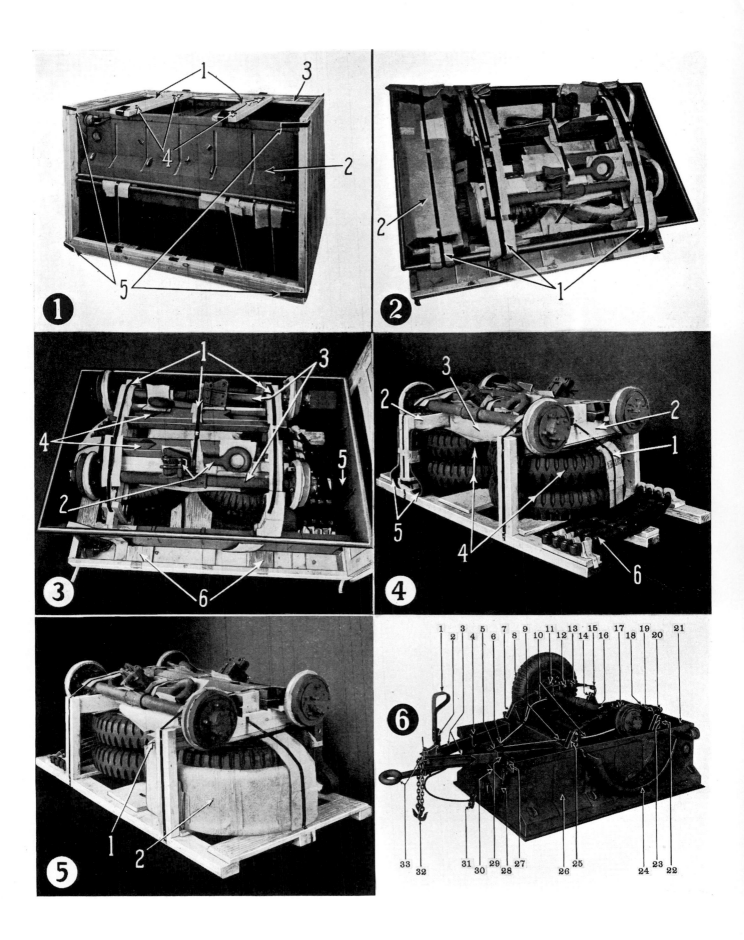

Acres of battle and accident damaged jeeps littered the landscape of a US Army salvage yard in France during WWII. The Government expected the average service life of a jeep in combat areas to be about 90 days.

This list of manufacturer abbreviations should be helpful to all MV enthusiasts. It is taken from the very rare three volume set of TMs, ORD 14-2 Interchange List for General Purpose and Combat Vehicles. The set of books contain nearly 3000 pages of valuable MV data.

Symbols	Manufacturer	Address

A

AAT	American Body and Trailer Company	Oklahoma City, Okla.
AB	Aetna Ball Bearing Mfg. Company	Chicago, Ill.
AC	A. C. Spark Plug Div. (GMC)	Flint, Mich.
ACB	American Coach & Body Company	Cleveland, Ohio
ACF	American Car & Foundry Co.	New York, N. Y.
AD	Alemite Div. (Stewart-Warner Corp.)	Chicago, Ill.
AHB	Ahlberg Bearing Company	Detroit, Mich.
AL	Electric Auto-Lite Company (The)	Toledo, Ohio
AM	Air-Maze Corp.	Philadelphia, Pa.
AMB	American Bantam Car Company	Butler, Pa.
AML	American Locomtive Company	Schenectady, N. Y.
AMR	American Roller Bearing Company	Pittsburgh, Pa.
ANC	Anthony Company, Inc.	Streator, Ill.
APD	Amplex Division (Chrysler Corp.)	Detroit, Mich.
AS	Allis-Chalmers Mfg. Company	Milwaukee 1, Wis.
ASC	American Seating Company	Grand Rapids, Mich.
AUC	Autocar Company	Ardmore, Pa.
AVM	Atwood Vacuum Machine Company	Rockford, Ill.
AY	Athey Truss Wheel Company	Indianapolis, Ind.

B

B&B	Borg & Beck Div. (Borg-Warner Corp.)	Rockford, Ill.
BCA	Bearings Company of America	Lancaster, Pa.
BDM	Biederman Motors Corp.	Cincinnati, Ohio
BDT	Black Diamond Trailer Co., Inc.	Bristol, Tenn.
BE	Buda Company (The)	Harvey, Ill.
BEB	Beebe Brothers	Seattle, Wash.
BG	B. G. Corp.	New York, N. Y.
BL	Brown Lipe Gear Co. (Spicer Mfg. Co.)	Toledo, Ohio
BLMA	Brake Lining Mfg. Ass'n.	
BLR	Ball & Roller Bearing Company	Danbury, Conn.
BLW	Baldwin Locomotive Works (The)	Philadelphia, Pa.
BM	Blood Brothers Machine Company	Allegan, Mich.
BMA	Anti-Friction Bearing Mfg. Ass'n.	New York, N. Y.
BMD	Buick Motor Div. (GMC)	Flint, Mich.
BN	Bantam Bearing Division	South Bend, Ind.
BNH	Ben Hur Mfg. Company	Milwaukee, Wis.
BO	American Bosch Corp.	Springfield, Mass.
BOW	Bower Roller Bearing Company	Detroit, Mich.
BRA	Braden Winch Company	Tulsa, Okla.
BRO	Brockway Motor Company, Inc.	Cortland, N. Y.
BRW	Borg-Warner Corp. (The)	Chicago, Ill.
BS	Bendix Stromberg Carburetor Co.	South Bend, Ind.
BV	Brill Co. J. G.	Philadelphia, Pa.
BW	Budd Wheel Company	Detroit, Mich.
BWE	Bendix-Westinghouse Automotive Air Brake Company	Elyria, Ohio
BX	Bendix Products Division	South Bend, Ind.
BXC	Bendix Aviation Corp.	Detroit, Mich.

C

CAD	Cadillac Motor Car Div. (GMC)	Detroit, Mich.
CAN	Candler-Hill Corp.	Detroit, Mich.
CAR	Carter Carburetor Corp.	St. Louis, Mo.
CAT	Caterpiller Tractor Company	Peoria, Ill.
CB	Corcoran-Brown Lamp Division (Electric Auto-Lite Lamp Co.)	Cincinnati, Ohio
CC	Chrysler Corp.	Detroit, Mich.
CCM	Checker Cab Mfg. Company	Kalamazoo, Mich.

CE	Clark Equipment Company	Buchanan, Mich.
CEC	Chandler Evans Corp.	South Meriden, Conn.
CEN	Century Boat Company	Manistee, Mich.
CH	Cutler-Hammer, Inc.	Milwaukee, Wis.
CLE	Cletrac Tractor Co. (The Cleveland Tractor)	Cleveland, Ohio
CM	Chicago Rawhide Mfg. Company	Chicago, Ill.
CMC	Coleman Motors Corp.	Littleton, Colo.
CME	Caterpillar Military Engine Company	Decatur, Ill.
CNP	Central Fibre Products Company	Chelsea, Mich.
CO	Continental Motors Corp.	Muskegon, Mich.
COR	Corbitt Company (The)	Henderson, N. C.
CP	Champion Spark Plug Company	Toledo, Ohio
CRB	Corbin Div. (The American Hardware Corp.)	New Britain, Conn.
CSP	Cleveland Steel Products Corp.	Cleveland, Ohio
CTC	Carolina Truck & Trailer Company	Charlotte, N. C.
CTR	Carter Mfg. Company	Memphis, Tenn.
CU	Cuno Engineering Corp.	Meriden, Conn.
CUM	Cushman Motor Works	Lincoln, Neb.
CV	Chevrolet Motor Div. (GMC)	Detroit, Mich.
CWR	Continental-Built Wright Engine Parts (Continental Motors Corp.)	Detroit, Mich.

D

DA	Delco Appliance Div. (GMC)	Rochester, N. Y.
DAR	Dart Truck Company	Kansas City, Mo.
DAV	Davis Trailer Company (Davis Welding & Mfg. Co.)	Cincinnati, Ohio
DAW	Dayton Wheel Company	Dayton, Ohio
DAY	Dayton Rubber Mfg. Company	Dayton, Ohio
DDE	Detroit Diesel Engine Div. (GMC)	Detroit, Mich.
DDG	Dodge Brothers Corp. (Div. of Chrysler Corp.)	Detroit, Mich.
DH	Detroit Harvester Company	Detroit, Mich.
DM	Douglas Mfg. Co., H. A.	Bronson, Mich.
DN	Donaldson Company, Inc.	St. Paul, Minn.
DP	Delco Products Div. (GMC)	Dayton Ohio
DR	Delco-Remy Div. (GMC)	Anderson, Ind.
DRB	Dorsey Brothers	Elba, Ala.
DT	Diamond T Motor Car Company	Chicago, Ill.
DTD	Detroit Transmission Div. (GMC)	Detroit, Mich.
DWC	Differential Wheel Corp.	Detroit, Mich.
DWE	Davis Welding & Mfg. Company	Cincinnati, Ohio
DX	Deluxe Products Corp. (The)	Lake St. La Porte, Ind.
DZ	Dietz Company, R. E.	New York, N. Y.

E

EAL	E. A. Laboratories, Inc.	Brooklyn, N. Y.
EAT	Eaton Mfg. Co. (The)	Cleveland, Ohio
EC	Eclipse-Pioneer Div. (Bendix Aviation Corp.)	Teterboro, N. J.
ECM	Eclipse Machine Div. (Bendix Aviation Corp.)	Elmira, N. Y.
ED	Edison Storage Battery Division (Thos. A. Edison Inc.)	West Orange, N. J.
EDW	Edwards Iron Works, Inc.	South Bend, Ind.
ERM	Erie Malleable Iron Company	Erie, Pa.
ES	Exide Battery (Electric Storage Battery Company)	Philadelphia, Pa.
EV	Evans Appliance Co. (Candler-Hill Corp.)	Detroit, Mich.

F

FAF	Fafnir Bearing Company (The)	New Britain, Conn.
FB	Federal Bearings Co. Inc.	Poughkeepsie, N. Y.
FDM	Federal Mogul Corp.	Detroit, Mich.
FE	Federal Electric Company	Chicago, Ill.
FF	Fruehauf Trailer Company	Detroit, Mich.
FH	Fisher Tank Div. (GMC)	Detroit, Mich.
FHB	Fisher Body Div. (GMC)	Detroit, Mich.
FM	Ford Motor Company	Dearborn, Mich.
FMT	Federal Motor Truck Company	Detroit, Mich.
FN	Fitzgerald Mfg. Company	Torrington, Conn.
FOM	Food Machinery Corp.	San Jose, Calif.
FR	Fram Corp.	Providence, R. I.
FSN	Federal Stock Number	
FT	Firestone Tire & Rubber Company	Akron, Ohio
FTB	Firestone Battery Company (Subsd. Firestone Tire & Rubber Co.)	Akron, Ohio
FTC	Fontaine Truck Equipment Co.	Birmingham, Ala.
FUL	Fuller Mfg. Company	Kalamazoo, Mich.
FWD	Four Wheel Drive Auto Company	Clintonville, Wis.

G

GAB	Galion Allsteel Body Company (The)	Galion, Ohio
GE	General Electric Company	Schenectady, N. Y.
GEM	Gemmer Mfg. Company	Detroit, Mich.
GER	Gerwtenslager Company (The)	Wooster, Ohio
GK	Gabriel Company (The)	Cleveland, Ohio
GL	Guide Lamp Div. (GMC)	Anderson, Ind.
GLU	Globe-Union, Inc. (Centralab Div.)	Milwaukee, Wis.
GM	General Motors Corp.	Detroit, Mich.
GPC	Garlock Packing Company (The)	New York, N. Y.
GPM	Graham-Paige Motors Corp.	Detroit, Mich.
GR	Goodrich Company, B. F. (The)	Akron, Ohio
GT	Goodyear Tire & Rubber Co. Inc.	Akron, Ohio
GTT	Gramm Truck & Trailer Corp.	Delphos, Ohio
GU	Guiberson Diesel Engine Company	Dallas, Texas
GV	Gates Rubber Co. (The) ("Gates-Vulco")	Denver, Colo.
GW	Gar Wood Industries, Inc.	Detroit, Mich.

H

HA	Handy Governor Div. (King-Seeley Corp.)	Ann Arbor, Mich.
HAC	Hall Lamp Company, C. M.	Detroit, Mich.
HBB	Hobbs Corp., J. W.	Springfield, Ill.
HC	Cole-Hersee Company	Boston, Mass.
HE	Houde Engineering Corp.	Buffalo, N. Y.
HEB	Hercules Body Company, Inc.	Evansville, Ind.
HEN	Henney Motor Company	Freeport, Ill.
HGB	Highland Body Mfg. Company (Trailer Company of America)	Cincinnati, Ohio
HJ	Hyde Trailer Company	Fort Worth, Texas
HL	Homelite Corp.	Port Chester, N. Y.
HLC	Heil Company (The)	Milwaukee, Wis.
HLS	Hall-Scott Motor Car Company	Berkeley, Calif.
HM	Hercules Motors Corp.	Canton, Ohio
HO	Hoover Ball & Bearing Company	Ann Arbor, Mich.
HOF	Hoof Products Company	Chicago, Ill.
HOL	Holley Carburetor Company	Detroit, Mich.
HRD	Harley-Davidson Motor Company	Milwaukee, Wis.
HSP	Hercules Steel Products Company	Galion, Ohio
HY	Hyatt Bearings Div. (GMC)	Harrison, N. J.
HZ	Heinze Electric Company (Div. of Consolidated Electric Lamp Co.)	Lowell, Mass.

I

IB	Imperial Brass Mfg. Co. (The)	Chicago, Ill.
IHC	International Harvester Company, Inc.	Chicago, Ill.
IMC	Indian Motorcycle Company	Springfield, Mass.
IMD	Inland Mfg. Div. (GMC)	Dayton, Ohio
IMP	Independent Metal Products Company	Omaha, Neb.
IWC	Industrial Wire Cloth Products Corp.	Wayne, Mich.

J

JDC	Deere & Company, John	Moline, Ill.
JMS	Jones-Motrola Sales Company	Stanford, Conn.

K

KEC	Keystone Trailer & Equipment Company, Inc.	Kansas City, Mo.
KEM	Kentucky Mfg. Corp.	Louisville, Ky.
KHW	Kelsey Hayes Wheel Company	Detroit, Mich.
KMT	Kenworth Motor Truck Corp.	Seattle, Wash.
KS	King-Seeley Corp.	Ann Arbor, Mich.
KSS	Krieger Co. (Krieger Steel Sections, Inc.)	Long Island City, N. Y.
KTC	Kingham Trailer Company	Louisville, Ky.

L

LGT	Ligget Spring & Axle Co.	E. Monongahela, Pa.
LI	Lisle Corp.	Clarinda, La.
LK	Link-Belt Company	Chicago, Ill.
LLM	L & L Mfg. Company	Indianapolis, Ind.
LM	Long Mfg. Div. (Borg-Warner Corp.)	Detroit, Mich.
LMD	Long Mfg. Div. (Borg-Warner Corp.)	Detroit, Mich.
LN	Leece-Neville Company	Cleveland, Ohio
LO	Wagner Electric Corp.	St. Louis, Mo.
LP	Logansport Machine Co., Inc.	Logansport, Ind.
LPC	La Plante-Choate Mfg. Co., Inc.	Cedar Rapids, La.
LPE	Lipe-Rollway Corp.	Syracuse, N. Y.
LY	Lycoming Div. (Aviation Corp.)	Williamsport, Pa.

M

MAE	Monroe Auto Equipment Company	Monroe, Mich.
MAR	Maremont Automotive Products, Inc.	Chicago, Ill.
MBC	Miffinburg Body Works, Inc.	Miffinburg, Pa.
MCH	Michigan Leather Packing Company	Detroit, Mich.
MG	McGill Mfg. Company, Inc.	Valparaiso, Ind.
MH	Marmon-Herrington Co. Inc.	Indianapolis, Ind.
MIR	Miller Auto Cruiser Trailer Co., A. J.	Bradenton, Fla.
MJ	Mechanics Universal Joint Division (Borg-Warner Corp.)	Rockford, Ill.
M	Mack Mfg. Corp.	New York, N. Y.
MM	Moto Meter Gauge & Equipment Division (Electric Auto-Lite Corp.)	Toledo, Ohio
MMP	Minneapolis Moline Power Implement Co.	Minneapolis, Minn.
MP	Monmouth Products Company	Cleveland, Ohio
MPC	Michiana Products Corp.	Michigan City, Ind.
MRC	Marlin-Rockwell Corp.	Jamestown, N. Y.
MRM	Manhattan Rubber Mfg. Co.	Passaic, N. J.
MSCC	Marvel-Schebler Carburetor Corp.	Flint, Mich.
MW	Motor Wheel Corp.	Lansing, Mich.
MY	Massey-Harris Co. (Tank Div.)	Racine, Wis.

N

NBR	Nabors Company, W. C.	Mansfield, La.
NC	Nice Ball Bearing Company	Philadelphia, Pa.
ND	New Departure Div. (GMC)	Bristol, Conn.
NH	Norma-Hoffman Bearing Corp.	Stanford, Conn.
NI	Novi Equipment Company	Novi, Mich.
NK	Nash-Kelvinator Corp. (Nash Motors Div.)	Kenosha, Wis.
NMB	National Motor Bearing Company, Inc.	Redwood City, Calif.
NP	New Process Gear, Inc.	Syracuse, N. Y.
NPN	No Part Number	

OCL	W. G. B. Oil Clarifer, Inc.	Kingston, N. Y.
OEL	Oneida, Ltd.	Canastota, N. Y.
OG	Oilgear Company (The)	Milwaukee, Wis.
OKS	Oakes Products Div. (Houdaille-Hershey)	Detroit, Mich.
OL	Olson Mfg. Company	Delco, Idaho
OMT	Oshkosh Motor Truck Inc.	Oshkosh, Wis.
ORB	Orange Roller Bearing Company	Orange, N. J.
ORD	Ordnance Department	
OSN	Official Stock Number	
OT	Omaha Standard Body Corp.	Council Bluffs, Iowa

P

PAC	Packard Motor Car Company	Detroit, Mich.
PC	Packard Electric Div. (GMC)	Warren, Ohio
PF	Pacific Car & Foundry Company	Seattle, Wash.
PG	Pierce Governor Company	Anderson, Ind.
PKC	Pike Trailer Company	Los Angeles, Calif.
PL	Prest-O-Lite Storage Battery Co., Inc.	Indianapolis, Ind.
PM	Pullman Standard Car Mfg. Co.	Chicago, Ill.
PMC	Plymouth Motor Corp.	Detroit, Mich.
PMD	Pontiac Motor Div. (GMC)	Pontiac, Mich.
POW	Pointer-Willamette Company	Portland, Ore.
PRM	Progress Mfg. Company	Arthur, Ill.
PRS	Pressed Steel Car Co., Inc.	Pittsburgh, Pa.
PSB	Perfection Steel Body Company (The)	Galion, Ohio
PU	Purolator Products, Inc.	Newark, N. J.

Q

QC	Queen City Trailer Company	Cincinnati, Ohio

R

RB	Roller Bearing Company of America	Trenton, N. J.
RBC	Rogers Brothers Corp.	Albion, Pa.
RC	Reo Motors, Inc.	Lansing, Mich.
RD	Rockford Drilling Machine Div.	Rockford, Ill.
RE	Romec Pump Company	Elyria, Ohio
RET	Reliance Trailer & Truck Company, Inc.	San Francisco, Calif.
RG	Ross Gear & Tool Company	Lafayette, Ind.
ROC	Rockford Mfg. Company	Rockford, Tenn.
RU	Redman Trailer Company	Alma, Mich.

S

SAC	Shuler Axle Company, Inc.	Louisville, Ky.
SCI	Scintilla Magneto Division	Sidney, N. Y.
SD	Studebaker Corp. (The)	South Bend, Ind.
SDW	Springfield Wagon & Trailer	Springfield, Mo.
SFA	Standard Forge & Axle Co., Inc.	Montgomery, Ala.
SG	Shafer Bearing Corp.	Chicago, Ill.
SHB	Streich & Brothers Company	Oshkosh, Wis.
SK	Shakeproof Lock Washer Company	Chicago, Ill.
SKC	Strick Company	Philadelphia, Pa.
SKF	SKF Industries, Inc.	Philadelphia, Pa.
SLV	St. Louis Car Company	St. Louis, Mo.
SOM	Super Oil Seal Mfg. Company	Dearborn, Mich.
SP	Spicer Mfg. Corp.	Toledo, Ohio
SPD	Speedometer Shop (The)	North Seattle, Wash.
SPE	Spencer Trailer Company	Angusta, Kansas
SPG	Sperry Gyroscope Company, Inc.	Brooklyn, N. Y.
SPW	Sparks-Withington Company (The)	Jackson, Mich.
SS	Saginaw Stamping & Tool Co.	Saginaw, Mich.
SSG	Saginaw Steering Gear Division (GMC)	Saginaw, Mich.
STE	Snyder Tool & Engineering Co.	Detroit, Mich.
STL	Steel Products Company, Inc. (The)	Savannah, Ga.
STS	Standard Seal Company (National Motor Bearing Company, Inc.)	Van Wert, Ohio

SUT	Superior Trailer Mfg. Corp.	Indianapolis, Ind.
SW	Stewart-Warner Corp.	Chicago, Ill.
SZE	Schwarze Electric Company	Adrian, Michigan

T

TC	Twin Disc Clutch Company	Racine, Wis.
TCA	Trailmobile Company (The) (Formerly Trailer Co. of America)	Cincinnati, Ohio
TCC	Travelcar Corp. (The)	Detroit, Mich.
TCO	Trailco Mfg. & Sales Co.	Hummels Wharf, Pa.
TD	Timken-Detroit Axle Co. (The)	Detroit, Mich.
TEB	Timpte Brothers	Denver, Colo.
TIM	Timken Roller Bearing Co. (The)	Canton, Ohio
TJ	Thermoid Company	Trenton, N. J.
TL	Tillotson Mfg. Company (The)	Toledo, Ohio
TN	Truck Engineering Corp.	Cleveland, Ohio
TR	Torrington Company (The)	Torrington, Conn.
TRI	Trico Products Corp.	Buffalo, N. Y.
TRU	American Chain & Cable Company (Tru-Stop) (Hazard Wire Rope Div.)	Wilkes-Barre, Pa.
TU	Tulsa Winch Mfg. Corp.	Tulsa, Okla.
TV	Transportation Equipment Co.	New Orleans, La.
TWS	Thew Shovel Company (The)	Lorain, Ohio
TX	Tyson Bearing Corp.	Massillon, Ohio

U

UN	Universal Oil-Seal Company	Pontiac, Mich.
UP	Universal Products Company, Inc.	Dearborn, Mich.
UR	Utility Trailer Mfg. Company	Los Angeles, Calif.
USL	USL Battery Corp. (Auto-Lite Battery Corp.)	Niagara Falls, N. Y.
UTS	United Specialties Company	Chicago, Ill.

V

VG	Victor Mfg. & Gasket Company	Chicago, Ill.
VR	Vortox Mfg. Company	Claremont, Calif.

W

WAL	Walter Motor Truck Co.	Ridgewood, L. I., N. Y.
WB	Willard Storage Battery Company	Cleveland, Ohio
WBK	Westinghouse Air Brake Co., Industrial Div.	Wilmerding, Pa.
WE	Westinghouse Electric & Mfg. Co.	E. Pittsburgh, Pa.
WEB	Warner Electric Brake Mfg. Company	Beloit, Wis.
WF	Ward LaFrance Truck Division (Great American Industries)	Elmira, N. Y.
WG	Warner Gear Div. (Borg-Warner Corp.)	Muncie, Ind.
WGC	Woodward Governor Company	Rockford, Ill.
WH	Weatherhead Company (The)	Cleveland, Ohio
WHK	Whitehead & Kales Company	River Rouge, Mich.
WHS	Watson Company, H. S.	San Francisco, Calif.
WI	White Motor Company (The)	Cleveland, Ohio
WIL	Wilcox-Rich (Div. of Eaton Mfg. Co.)	Detroit, Mich.
WIS	Wisconsin Axle Div. (Timken-Detroit Axle Company)	Oshkosh, Wis.
WKM	Waukesha Motor Company	Waukesha, Wis.
WM	Weaver Mfg. Company	Springfield, Ill.
WO	Willys-Overland Motors, Inc.	Toledo, Ohio
WR	Wright Aeronautical Corp.	Paterson, N. J.
WW	Winter-Weiss Company (The)	Denver, Colo.

Y

YT	GMC Truck & Coach (Div. GMC) (Formerly Yellow Truck & Coach Mfg. Co.)	Pontiac, Mich.

Z

Z	Zenith Carburetor Div. (Bendix Aviation Corp.)	Detroit, Mich.

NOTES AND CORRECTIONS

Page 156:
Houdak is correctly spelled Hudak.

Page 167:
The photo was made in Belgium and not in Greece.

Page 182:
The total production of GPs should be shown as 4458.

Page 183:
The number under NOV. 1941 should be 145. The grand total should be 226587.

Page 185:
MB 400767 was delivered December 24, 1944. MB 436653 is really 430653.

Page 187:
GPW 78228 was delivered November 10, 1942.

Page 239:
The jeep rope should be 24 feet (7.3 m) long.

CORRECTIONS & AMPLIFICATIONS
VOLUME I OF ALL-AMERICAN WONDER

It is a difficult task to assemble a lot of data from a wide variety of written and verbal sources, write it down, have it typeset and produce a book on the technical subject without having errors in the printed version. Many of the errors in Volume I of this book are corrected in the text, illustrations and captions of Volume II. The list that follows is additional corrections to Volume I.

Page 4:
The first word in the first line is of course, misspelled. Spelling is obviously not my strong suit.

Page 9:
The work FOREWARD should be FOREWORD. Book one got off to a pretty rough start.

Page 25:
It is certain that some Ford bodies also came with caged nuts (G Smith).

Page 38
Photo number 10 is a picture from a totally different series than the other 9 pictures preceding it. Number 10 was taken at Rockhampton, Queensland, Australia on 24 August 1943 (D Miller).

Page 38:
The last paragraph of text on Lend-Lease was largely assumption on my part, proved incorrect by subsequent research contained in the Czechoslovakian section of Volume II.

Page 39:
Nomenclature plates are also commonly found made from steel and many typesetting variations exist.

Page 60:
Column 3, second paragraph, first line, word *Origination* should be Organization (D Spence).

Page 63:
FSMWO-G503-W5 should say 2-6v batteries, gen, PTO (L Fleckenstein).

Page 69-70:
The serial number list contains several errors and should be abandoned in favor of the list in volume II (be careful! There may be errors in the new list as well).

Page 70:
It is also correct for serial numbers on Ford frames to be placed on the left frame rail *ahead* of the crossmember (C Th Verschure).

Page 70:
Willys chassis serial number plates were also made of zinc. As reported in this book many early Ford GPWs were built on Willys frames (D Miller).

Page 75:
The late hood block shown in the drawings was also used on the early MBs and after the war on the CJ-2A.

Page 83:
The switch depicted was not made by Klixon. Only the thermal circuit breaker is a Klixon. The switch is a Douglas (J J Wislon).

Page 85:
After item 63F and 64W there should be a notation to see the drawing at the bottom of page 95 for details.

Page 86:
Rubber *or* felt grommets may be used in holes 90, 37 and 62 in the top drawing.

Page 88:
It should be noted that the chain used is know as "single-jack" chain.

Page 90:
Holes 24, 25, 21, 20, 22, 23, 19, 18, 17, 16 and f, g. h, i and j on both drawings are placed too far to the right. All 15 should be moved 1/2 inch (12mm) to the left (R Hodgson).

Page 97
The blackout lamps illustrated are really part number A-1436 (left) or A-1437 (right) and apparently the type shown as GPW is the early variety and the one shown as MB is the later production.

Page 109:
Regarding BO driving lights, it should have been mentioned that these were not used at all on jeeps until about August of 1942. From Mid Series Production both the MB and GPW used the more radically curved bracket (Y Ohtsuka).

Page 109:
The drawing shown as Ford is actually both Ford and Willys *early* body construction. The one labeled as Willys is the improved construction common to both the GPW and MB (D Miller).

Page 111:
The square recess around the tool box lock shown on the GPW illustration was used only on pure Ford bodies up until the introduction of the composite body, probably late in 1943 (T Sudds).

Page 113:
The drawing of the Ford spring clip should have a hole through the center of the bottom (Y Ohtsuka).

Page 117:
Actually both types of windshield studs were common to the MB and GPW. The early ones used the push bottom type and the later ones used the A-4120 (D Miller).

Page 118:
The measurements of the gas can strap are reversed. The portion with the buckle on it is the shorter of the two.

Page 122:
This drawing and caption are too presumptuous. There seems to be an almost random use of the two styles on both MBs and GPWs in VEP and EP jeeps.

Page 124:
The bottom of the top bow swivel bracket in the drawing should be pointed rather than flat (C Th Verschure).

Page 126:
Other marks found on Willys bolt heads are AA, EC, C/TR, etc.

Page 134:
Tappet clearances shown as hot — should be *cold* (J Arnold).

Page 139:
Ford clutch inspection covers can also be found with two round holes like the typical MB cover.

Page 140:
The last entry regarding mufflers should be followed by the date of May 1942 rather than March 1942 (J Nemeth).

I should finish this section on corrections by saying I'm not in the least "thin skinned" about criticism. Quite the contrary. If you see a mistake in this book, I would welcome a correction of it. That is how we all achieve knowledge. I have no predisposition to proving my conclusions are correct, but rather look forward to seeing anyone's conclusion documented.

Finally, the little cards shown on page 30 of Volume I of this book (page 43 of the revised edition) have been reprinted thousands of times and read by jeep freaks all over the world. On those cards I offered a lot of money if someone would find an original WWII jeep in a crate for me. Needless to say, none has turned up in over 10 years that the offer has run.

THE   END

© COPYRIGHT
1986
RRC

For a complete list of military vehicle books published by USM, write:
USM, MV
Box 810
Lakeville, MN 55044-0810
USA